# FROM RAGS TO RICKETTS

# Borgo Press Books by WILLIAM L. SLOUT

*Amphitheatres and Circuses: A History from Their Earliest Date to 1861, with Sketches of Some of the Principal Performers*, by Col. T. Allston Brown (editor)
*Broadway Below the Sidewalk: Concert Saloons of Old New York* (editor)
*Broadway's Poor Relation: Plays and Players of Repertoire and Stock, 1920-1930*
*The Burial of Alma: A Comedy in Two Acts*
*Burnt Cork and Tambourines: A Source Book for Negro Minstrelsy* (editor)
*Chilly Billy: The Evolution of a Circus Millionaire*
*Clowns and Cannons: The American Circus During the Civil War*
*En Route to the Great Eastern Circus and Other Essays on Circus History*
*From Rags to Ricketts and Other Essays on Circus History*
*Fun and Fancy in Old New York: Selections from a Series, "Reminiscences of a Man about Town,"* by Col. Tom Picton (editor)
*Grand Entrée: The Birth of the Greatest Show on Earth, 1870-1875* (with Stuart L. Thayer)
*Ink from a Circus Press Agent: An Anthology of Circus History from the Pen of Charles H. Day*, by Charles H. Day (editor)
*Joe Blackburn's A Clown's Log, Second Edition*, by Charles H. Day (editor)
*Life Upon the Wicked Stage: A Visit to the American Theatre of the 1860s, 1870s, and 1880s As Seen in the Pages of the New York Clipper* (editor)
*Old Gotham Theatricals: Selections from a Series, "Reminiscences of a Man about Town,"* by Col. Tom Picton (editor)
*Olympians of the Sawdust Circle: A Biographical Dictionary of the Nineteenth-Century American Circus*
*Popular Amusements in Horse & Buggy America: An Anthology of Contemporaneous Essays* (editor)
*A Royal Coupling: The Historic Marriage of Barnum and Bailey*
*Theatre in a Tent: The Development of Provincial Entertainment*
*The Theatrical Rambles of Mr. and Mrs. John Greene*, Second Edition, by Charles Durang (editor)
*The Trial of Dr. Jekyll: An Adaptation of Robert Louis Stevenson's "The Strange Case of Dr. Jekyll and Mr. Hyde": A Play in Two Acts*

# FROM RAGS TO RICKETTS

## AND OTHER ESSAYS ON CIRCUS HISTORY

WILLIAM L. SLOUT

THE BORGO PRESS
MMXII

**Clipper Studies in the Theatre**
ISSN 0748-237X

Number Twenty-One

FROM RAGS TO RICKETTS

Copyright © 1997, 1998, 1999, 2000, 2012 by
William L. Slout

FIRST EDITION

Published by Wildside Press LLC

www.wildsidebooks.com

# FROM RAGS TO RICKETTS

# CONTENTS

ACKNOWLEDGMENTS . . . . . . . . . . . . . . .9
FROM RAGS TO RICKETTS: The Roots of
   Circus in Early Gotham. . . . . . . . . . . . 11
THE GREAT ROMAN HIPPODROME OF 1874:
   P. T. Barnum's "Crowning Effort" . . . . . . . 29
THE RECYCLING OF THE DAN RICE PARIS
   PAVILION CIRCUS . . . . . . . . . . . . . . 45
STRANGE BEDFELLOWS: The Pogey O'Brien
   Interval, 1874-1875 . . . . . . . . . . . . . . 75
TWO RINGS AND A HIPPODROME TRACK. . 93
THE ADVENTURES OF JAMES M. NIXON,
   FORGOTTEN IMPRESARIO . . . . . . . . 103
ABOUT THE AUTHOR. . . . . . . . . . . . . 203

# ACKNOWLEDGMENTS

These essays have been previously published as follows, and are published by arrangement with the author:

"From Rags to Ricketts: The Roots of the Circus in Early Gotham" was published in *Bandwagon: The Journal of the Circus Historical Society, Inc.*, Vol. 48, No. 5 (September-October, 2004), p. 28-32. Copyright © 2004, 2012 by William L. Slout.

"The Great Roman Hippodrome of 1874: P. T. Barnum's 'Crowning Effort'" was published in *Bandwagon: The Journal of the Circus Historical Society, Inc.*, Vol. 42, No. 1 (January-February, 1998), p. 29-34. Copyright © 1998, 2012 by William L. Slout.

"The Recycling of the Dan Rice Paris Pavilion Circus" was presented at the 1998 Circus Historical Society Convention in Atlanta, Georgia, and was published in *Bandwagon: The Journal of the Circus Historical Society, Inc.*, Vol. 42, No. 4 (July-August, 1998), p. 13-21. Copyright © 1998, 2012 by William L. Slout.

"Strange Bedfellows: The Pogey O'Brien Interval, 1874-1875" was published in *Bandwagon: The Journal of the Circus Historical Society, Inc.*, Vol. 43, No. 4

(July-August, 1999), p. 21-25. Copyright © 1999, 2012 by William L. Slout.

"Two Rings and a Hippodrome Track" was presented at the 2000 Circus Historical Society Convention, and was published in *Bandwagon: The Journal of the Circus Historical Society, Inc.*, Vol. 44, No. 6 (November-December, 2000), p. 18-23. Copyright © 2000, 2012 by William L. Slout.

"The Adventures of James M. Nixon, Forgotten Impresario" was published in *Bandwagon: The Journal of the Circus Historical Society, Inc.*, Vol. 41, No. 4 (July-August, 1997), p. 4-14; Vol. 41, No. 5 (September-October, 1997), p. 16-23; Vol. 41, No. 6 (November-December, 1997), p. 44-51. Copyright © 1997, 2012 by William L. Slout.

# FROM RAGS TO RICKETTS
## The Roots of Circus in Early Gotham

Early performances in the city of New York have been reported in various sources over the years, so revealing them here is not original. Rather, the objective within these pages is to place events into a sequence that reveals the progressive nature and increasing popularity of entertainments, as populations increase and the city expands from the Battery and moves up town.

A century before the canvas pavilion was adopted for exhibition purposes showmen relied on semi-permanent or permanent structures for such use. The temporary venues were just that, and, like anything temporary, the life span was short. Permanent buildings, on the other hand, are a symbol of longevity, reassurance that something important has been established. For example, during the latter half of the nineteenth-century, when expanding railroad mileage westward created new towns and cities, one of the first buildings that legitimized their existence was an opera house or theatre. So it is logical that we begin our New York narrative with just that.

The first permanent structure for public amusement viewing in New York was a theatre. Opened on December 6, 1732, it was a primitive affair built by Rip Van Dam, a bulbous Dutchman who owned a warehouse at Maiden Lane and Pearl Street, at the tip of Manhattan, adjacent to Fort George, the loft of which he converted for theatrical use.

Van Dam was a native of Albany. He moved to New York City and became a wealthy merchant and shipowner, and for many years served on the city counsel, during which time he sired fifteen children.

His converted loft appears to have been called the New Theatre, which might suggest there was an old one somewhere; but I do not believe that to be a fact. It seated about 300 spectators, who squatted on benches and watched the proceedings by dim candlelight. The only stove, being in the makeshift lobby, was a fire hazard and of so little use that during really cold weather the patrons brought foot warmers to survive the lengthy programs. An indication of the comportment of the clientele was a sign that urged them not to spit.[1] This early temple of drama existed only a year or two. It will be after the Revolution before other permanent houses of entertainment are established.

At the beginning of the eighteenth-century the economy of New York was in the midst of an upsurge, primarily due to the exporting of sugar to England. What had been a luxury only the privileged could

---

1. Edward Robb Ellis, *The Epic of New York City* (New York: Kodansha International, 1997), p. 119..

afford in the previous century, the British consumption of sugar had at least doubled by 1730 due to improved purchasing power and falling prices. Now it was a daily ritual of middle-class life to partake of sweetened chocolate or coffee, accompanied by candies, cakes or bread spread with molasses. The British sweet-tooth had sweetened the pocketbooks of New York merchants. With this, the city saw an expansion of trade in other areas as well. Between 1694 and 1720 over fifty new tavern-keepers, grocers and wine-sellers were granted licenses. New inns provided housing for seamen and business travelers. Retail shops also boomed.[2]

Yet there was a wide divide between the "haves" and "have-nots," and by 1730 a depression was taking root. There were some 8,600 people living in the city at this time, but a mere 140 merchants and landowners owned half the taxable wealth. One third of the white population was destitute.[3] It is little wonder, then, that traveling exhibitions were slow to develop.

There were, however, some eighteenth-century circus forerunners that offered entertainments and exhibitions which early-on took the place of museums, menageries, mechanics fairs and hall shows, presented at such sites as taverns, storefronts, open fields or city squares. Booth shows with small collapsible stages were erected on the street, in the smallest of buildings, by the seaside, or most any place people were in the habit of congregating. These were the type of amuse-

2. Edwin G. Burrows and Mike Wallace, *Gotham, a History of New York City to 1898* (New York: Oxford University Press, 1999), p. 119-124.

3. *Ibid.*, p. 151.

ments that could be easily transported from place to place on horseback or by small wagon, or even on the back of a single operator.

Mechanical wonders were popular items of display for which admission was charged. There was a man named Blanchard who revealed a carriage that was made to run without horses, described as an automaton eagle which, when guided by a passenger, could move at the speed of a stagecoach. There were scientific phenomena such as a way of electrifying several persons at the same time so fire darted from all parts of their bodies; or a contrivance that created by luminous rays the thirteen stars of the United States, and other pieces of artificial fireworks. There was even something called a "philosophical optical machine." Barnum must have loved the thought of them all.

Forerunners of the menagerie date as far back as 1728 when New Yorkers were exposed to a lion at the Jamaica Fair. The fair was originated this year as a site for selling merchandize and fine horses.

In 1733 a camel was on exhibit at the sign of the Cart and Horse. An item in the *Gazette* read:

> "NOTICE is hereby given to all Persons, that there is come to Town, a very Wonderful and Surprising Creature to all Persons in these Parts of the World; and it is in Scripture the very same Creature which is there called a CAMEL. It is impossible to describe the Creature; and therefore all Persons of ingenious Curiosity have an Opportunity of satisfying

themselves. The Creature was brought with great Difficulty from the Deserts of Arabia in that Quarter of the World which is called Asia to New England; a Curiosity which never was in this Country, and very likely will never be again."

The price of viewing was one shilling for adults and six pence for children.[4] Of course the Curiosity was seen again; in fact a pair of them, when in 1787 they were housed for show at Stevens' Livery Stables on Wall Street.

Two years later New Yorkers viewed a collection of animals that included a male and female "Ourang Outang," a sloth, a baboon, an anteater, crocodile, lizard, swordfish, a variety of snakes, a tiger, buffalo, and a selection of birds. Sounds like a menagerie to me.

It was announced in June of 1739: "Soon will come to town the upright German Hans who understands several languages, the most ingenious Horse that ever was seen in this Country." It was trained to salute the spectators, find hidden objects, answer questions with the nod of the head, identify playing cards and commit other unusual tricks, this act being shared with a clown.[5] A trained animal and a clown—at least the beginning of a circus program.

---

4. George C. D. Odell, *Annals of the New York Stage, Vol. I* (New York: Columbia University Press, 1927), p. 18?.

5. *Ibid.*

We learn of the appearance of a many-talented Anthony Joseph Dugee, who, in 1752, arranged to perform in a new exhibition hall in Mr. Adam Van Denberg's Garden. Dugee cavorted on the slack-wire, balanced seven pipes on his nose, as well as a straw on the head of a drinking glass, juggled balls and danced the hornpipe. He was accompanied by Mrs. Dugee, billed as the female Samson because of her ability to extend her body between two chairs while a 300 pound anvil on her breast was struck with the sledge hammers of two men; and in the same position she stalwartly bore the weight of six men. Then, with an additional show of strength she lifted the anvil with her hair. Circus acts but not a circus.

It might also be noted that the first public pleasure grounds with the name of Vauxhall Garden was established in 1765 by Samuel Fraunces, a proprietor of various taverns. Although several summer gardens opened in the 1740s and 1750s, there were only two remaining at this time—Spring Garden and Catiemuts Garden. This new Vauxhall was located on a site overlooking the Hudson, near what is now a junction of Greenwich and Warren Streets. The place featured a wax museum, fireworks and afternoon teas. More gardens with the name of Vauxhall would appear later.[6]

---

6. Burrows and Wallace, 176. Joseph Delacroix opened a summer resort he called Vauxhall Garden in 1798, located just above Pine Street at 112 Broadway, where, for a small admission, patrons could buy ice cream or a glass of punch. The next year he purchased the property of Alderman Nicholas Bayard, up Broadway near Bunker's Hill. (The Bayards were connected with the Stuyvesants by marriage and were prominent and prosperous citizens. Their bouwerie was somewhere between 100 and 200

The rough distinction made between an early "circus" and a "riding exhibition" or "riding school" is that the former has additional acts of amusement along with the riding itself, making it, the circus, a multi-act entertainment. Nevertheless, pre-circus riding exhibi-

---

acres. In 1729, the Bayards erected a large building near City Hall as a sugar refinery. It was later, in 1773, turned into a tobacco factory. It was William Bayard, the refiner of sugar, along with James Jauncy and Abraham Mortier, who, in 1760, purchased Richmond Hill, whereon they build the large wooden structure.) This new place he also titled Vauxhall Garden. Here, patrons were served the usual delicacies and refreshing drinks as at the original site, along with music, fireworks and other entertainments; and there were two carriages that furnished accommodations of travel between these upper and lower gardens. But nothing stands still. Crowded out by the rapid growth of the city, Vauxhall moved uptown once again. The new construction became one of the early milestones in the development of amusement venues in the city. It coincided with the dawn of the new century and a population that had almost doubled in the last decade, the 1800 census reporting a total of 60, 515 residing in the city. Modeled after the one with the same name in London, with long avenues of paintings, terminating with scenic renditions of a moonlight view, a hermit's cave, and other attempts at startling effects. There were alleys of Chinese lanterns, flying dragons and other samples of illumination. There was a saloon and a concert hall where young ladies sang to the accompaniment of a piano. The latticed bowers, half concealed from sight by foliage, furnished with tables and chairs for the quiet consumption of ice cream and other delicacies, were chief attractions on the summer nights, where the daughters of well-to-do mechanics and substantial traders preferred to lounge with their admirers. (Vauxhall Gardens, London, a popular place of resort from the reign of Charles II almost to the end of the nineteenth century, was located on the Surrey side of the Thames, near Vauxhall Bridge. Originally called New Spring Gardens, they were developed around 1661. At first there were only a few walks and arbors where supper was served. It was remodeled and reopened on June, 7, 1732, with "every appointment possible." There were many rows of tall trees, paintings and statues, a music room with an orchestra of fifty musicians, rows of colorful lamps. In the middle of the garden were two semicircles in which small booths allowed patrons to sit and refresh themselves with wine, tea, coffee, or various delicacies. The Gardens were open every day except Sundays, from May till September.)

tions were, if nothing else, the roots of circus performance, for circus performances early-on featured riding above all else. Such names as Sharp, Foulks, Bates, Pool and Ricketts represent the demonstration of riding as a pre-circus activity in this country. Four of these gentlemen appeared in New York City.

It was announced in Gaine's *New York Gazette* that Mr. Foulks would exhibit his skills of horsemanship on Mondays, Wednesdays and Fridays, beginning the 20th of December, 1771, "at a convenient Place belonging to Mr. Joseph Bogart near the Windmill above the Slaughter House, in the Bowery." The Windmill referred to was located on the western part of the Bowery between Hester and St. Nicholas Streets. Tickets could be purchased for four shillings at the newspaper offices of Mr. Rivington and Mr. Gaine. The rider was said to have performed in England, Ireland and Scotland, so we can assume he was not native to this country. "If the weather should be bad," the announcement read, "the performance will be postponed to the next fair day," a confirmation that the event took place in an uncovered enclosure. Foulks went through a series of routines with one, two and three horses which through the years have become familiar equestrian acts. In spite of the winter weather, performances continued into January. The only rivaling entertainment appearing during those cold months seems to have been an evening of legerdemain, of cups, balls and cards, by a Peter Sourville.[7]

---

7. Isaac J. Greenwood, *The Circus, Its Origins and Growth Prior to 1835* (New York: Dunlap Society Publications, N.S., 5), p. 48-51.

Another equestrian, Jacob Bates, arrived in New York in the spring of 1773. According to Greenwood, Bates had performed "throughout the length and breadth of Europe," purportedly before many of the crowned heads. His portrait was drawn and engraved by G. P. Nusbiegel in 1766. It pictured him standing by his horse while in the background were examples of his various feats being performed in a plot of ground much larger than a ring and cordoned off by what appears to be a rope. Some spectators are standing and others are sitting astride their mounts, giving them a better view of the action. We learn from the *Gazette* that Bates' New York performances were set for 5 p.m. and that there would be "proper seating for the ladies and gentlemen." The tickets for what was called "the first place" went for one dollar each; for the "second place," which could have been standing room, for four shillings. The announcement included a special request that Mr. Bates would "take it as a particular Favour if Gentlemen will not suffer Dogs to come with them." The show of horsemanship that took place at the Bull's Head in the Bowery beginning on the 2nd of June represented a much more civilized time of year than his predecessor, to be sure.[8] The most interesting

---

8. The Bull's Head was one of the memorable eighteenth-century hostelries, frequented by the butchers and drovers, the place being located near the slaughter yards. A 1763 newspaper advertisement is quoted as follows: "The noted Inn and Tavern in the Bowery Lane at the sign of the Bull's Head (where the slaughter house is now kept), lately kept by Caleb Hyatt, is now occupied by Thomas Bayeaux who is well provided with all the conveniences for travellers." Richard Varian, a successful butcher and superintendent of the public slaughter house, was proprietor of the inn from 1770 until the outset of the Revolution. By 1796 the property had come into

part of this visit was the introduction to this country of "Billy Button, or The Taylor Riding to Brentford," the equestrian burlesque of a tailor's difficulty in his journey to meet with a customer. Bates' performances continued through the summer until finalizing on August 3rd, at which time the boards that formed his arena were offered for sale.⁹

We now take a hurdle over the next several years, during which entertainment possibilities were bleak due to the Revolutionary War and the strictures that were a by-product of it. In 1774 the First Continental

---

the possession of Henry Astor, another butcher by trade and man of wealth by industry and ingenuity. The Bull's Head continued to be a meeting place of butchers and drovers until 1826, when it was razed to make way for the Old Bowery Theatre.

9. Greenwood, *op. cit.*, p. 48-51.

Congress passed a resolution to suppress entertainments:

> "We will, in our several stations, encourage frugality, economy and industry, and promote agriculture, arts, and manufactures of this country, especially that of wool; and will discountenance and discourage every species of extravagance and dissipation, especially all horse racing, and all kinds of gaming, cockfighting, exhibition of shews, plays, and other expensive diversions and entertainments."

We pick up our narrative in 1786, when Mr. Pool, billed as the first American to indulge in feats of horsemanship, arrived in New York for exhibitions on Tuesdays and Fridays beginning September 21st. His program reflected much of what Bates had done; and, indeed, Pool may have been a student of Bates. The site of his riding was advertised to be on the hill near the Jewish Burial Ground. This would be in the vicinity of Chatham Square. At this time we have added to the program a band of music and a clown who entertained the ladies and gentlemen between the feats. Such an improvement would give Mr. Pool a chance to rest before his next equestrian challenge. The visit persisted until the 1st of November.[10] Still not a circus, but at least we have a *troupe* of entertainers.

Enter the famous John Bill Ricketts, whose American beginnings were similar to the previous

---
10. *Ibid.*, p. 61.

gentlemen, starting out with a riding school and riding exhibitions; but now, after having established himself in Philadelphia and elsewhere, and thereby adding acts to his equestrian program, he brings his troupe to Greenwich Street, near the Battery. Ricketts had an advantage over the previous equestrians due to population growth. At this time New York could boast of having over 33,000 residents, 5,000 more than Philadelphia.

Circus historian T. Allston Brown wrote of him in 1860:

> "John B. Ricketts, the proprietor, was a very gentlemanly and neat fellow in society and dressed in rather the English sporting style and was received with favor in the best circles. As a performer he never offended the eye by ungraceful postures or by the nude style of dressing that now prevails at the circus. His costumes were like that of the actors on the stage—pantalets, trunks full disposed, and neat cut jacket—which were sufficient to make ample display of his figure for all purposes of agility and grace."[11]

Ricketts' circus opened in New York August 7th, 1793, in a newly constructed arena, which, unlike his equestrian forerunners, was fully enclosed. Horsemanship and feats astride the running mounts were

---

11. T. Allston Brown, *Amphitheatres and Circuses*, Borgo Press (San Bernardino, CA, 1994), p. 17.

prominently featured in the programs, the kind that has become an inherent part of riding acts in the intervening years. However Ricketts' brother Francis was an acrobat, a Mr. Spinacuta was a rope-walker, a Mr. McDonald a clown and a boy named Strobach rode on Ricketts' shoulders in the "Flying Mercury," all adding up to "circus." An item in the New York *Daily Advertiser* suggested on August 10th that "the bleak blasts of the Hudson should no longer be avoided by the Beau Monde for you may yet see at the circus a collection of so much beauty, innocence and gaiety as ever appeared in any of the public ballrooms." Performances were given daily at 4:00 p.m. until November 4th, presumably terminating because the structure was not heated.[12] Thus ended the first of a series of visits by the historically famous company, a company that would singly "own" the circus rights to New York for the next four years.

There is an exception to this, an event that occurred the following year, when on September 10, 1794, an amusement credited to Thomas Swann opened near the Battery, where, Thayer suspects, was the site Ricketts had used. But was this really a circus? George C. D. Odell, the maestro chronicler of New York theatrical history, considered it more of a riding school. Still, there was at least a band of musicians, and by October 20th a troupe of dancing monkeys under the care of a Mr. Cressin. Most notably for posterity, however, there was an equestrienne, a Miss Johnson, billed as an

---

12. Stuart Thayer, *Annals of the American Circus*, Vol. I, p. 6.

American Lady, seemingly the first American of her gender to appear in the ring.[13] This was Swann's first and last stand—a swan song, if you'll allow me—for shortly he began a practice of veterinary medicine in Philadelphia.

Ricketts returned to New York City, opening on November 24th, very shortly after Swann's departure, to spend the winter season at a new location at the southwest corner of Broadway and Exchange Alley (formerly Garden Street). At this time a grand entry was included in the program, adding a touch of spectacle and creating a tradition that has persisted to this day. Mr. McDonald did a burlesque riding act and something called "Polander's Tricks"; Ricketts carried Master Long in the "Flying Mercury," there were pony races, and by early January a Mr. Embroise was offering Italian fireworks. Further, in March there was an act billed as "Indian chiefs" on horseback, which Thayer calls "the first example of a long association of American Indians, pseudo or otherwise, with the circus." The run closed with a benefit for the poor on April 21, 1795.[14]

From November through April seems like a long run for a city of now about 40,000 people,[15] presented with a program limited in its variety over such a lengthy period. Still, there was little in the way of public amusements during the winter. The only major competitor was the John Street Theatre, exclusive in

---

13. *Ibid.*, p. 7.

14. *Ibid.*, p. 8-9.

15, The 1790 census recorded a population of 33,131.

that it offered the higher class of drama. Perhaps a lack of competition, and the novelty for people unfamiliar with Ricketts' kind of entertainment, and a public obsession with and a dependence on horses, may be part of the answer.

Ricketts returned on September 16$^{th}$, but closed three days later because of an epidemic of yellow fever that ended any amusement activity for the month, perhaps disrupting his intentions of continuing through the winter again.

Yellow fever first hit New York in 1702 and reappeared almost annually well into the nineteenth century. It was an epidemic that continually interrupted popular entertainments, particularly in southern port cities like Charleston, New Orleans and Mobile.

At this time, 1795, New York authorities had been alerted that yellow fever was widespread in the West Indies; but in New York the summer, hot and humid as it was, showed no indication of a problem. It was noticed, however, that mosquitoes were more numerous than usual, especially in the southeastern part of the city. Then, in mid-July, a health officer summoned to attend three sick seamen aboard a vessel in the East River caught the disease and died eight days later. More cases were in evidence along the waterfront. Many of the wealthy residents sent their families out of town in August; and, when the number of cases increased by September, those remaining shut their businesses and left for Greenwich, Harlem, and other nearby villages, leaving thousands of unemployed laborers to fend for themselves. The epidemic continued through October until it tapered off due to the cool weather; but not before it had claimed a record 732 victims.[16]

The cold weather came and went before New Yorkers were privileged to attend more of the performances. The circus took up residency again at Broadway and Exchange Alley in May of 1796. Now it consisted of John Bill Ricketts, rider; William Sully, rider and clown; Francis Ricketts, acrobat; Mr. Reano, rope-walker; Mr. Langley, clown; and Mr. Spinacuta, rope-walker. Mrs. Spinacuta rode a two-horse act, "never before attempted by any female in America," later designated Roman riding. Performances were presented each Tuesday, Thursday and Saturday until July 29th; then, after a respite of two months, there were six more dates between September 21st and 30th.[17]

To create change, dramatic offerings were made as the season progressed. Most were on themes that were offshoots of English pantomime and fair-booth shows common at this time. They were not new to New Yorkers, however, for as early as 1739 a pantomime was presented in the city at Mr. Holt's Long Room titled *Harlequin and Scaramouch; or, The Spaniard Trick'd*, which could be seen for the admission price of five shillings.[18]

A new amphitheatre, located on the west side of Greenwich Street, just north of Rector, awaited Ricketts' next opening; which, according to the New

---

16. Burrows and Wallace, p. 357.

17. Thayer, *op. cit.*, p. 11-12.

18. Odell, I, p. 18, taken from the New York *Weekly Courier*.

York *Argus,* was delayed until March 16, 1797, because inclement weather had prevented the arrival of the horses. The new, circular structure, for the first time in this city, included a stage and scenery along with the ring. The two performing areas were not physically accessible to one another at this time. The stage was simply alternated with the ring when dramatic-type interludes were presented. By the end of April a coffee shop was added for the pleasure of the patrons. The season ended July 12, 1797; but the company revisited Greenwich Street for a brief stay of two weeks in December of 1798. With that, Ricketts was destined not to return to the city; and, paradoxically, the building he had occupied burned the following year.[19] And with this, our narrative comes to an end.

---

19. Thayer, *op. cit.*, p.15-16.

# THE GREAT ROMAN HIPPODROME OF 1874
## P. T. BARNUM'S "CROWNING EFFORT"

It was the morning of April 25, 1874. A grand parade, made up of valuable stock forwarded by P. T. Barnum from Europe hit the streets of New York City. The procession was promoting the opening of P. T. Barnum's New Roman Hippodrome which the newspaper advertisements were touting as "The Event of 1874," occupying an entire block bounded by Madison and Fourth Avenues and 26th and 27th Streets, "at an expense of nearly one million dollars"—the largest collection of living wild animals in the world, along with *The Congress of Nations*, described as "the most magnificent and dazzling spectacle ever witnessed in this country."[20] Amazingly, most of the puffery turned out to be the truth.

A Roman Hippodrome? Not a circus? How could this be, when P. T. Barnum's Great Museum, Menagerie, Hippodrome and Traveling World's Fair, which was

---
20. New York *Times*, April 24, 1874, p. 7.

indeed a circus, had just the year before fulfilled a record-breaking summer tour? Nevertheless, the attention of the Barnum organization was now focused on a "non-circus."

Since the Franconi Hippodrome was established in New York City in 1853, the use of the word "hippodrome" to describe a place of exhibition or form of entertainment appears on occasion in circus advertising; but there is nothing to suggest from this that any form of actual racing occurred around a hippodrome track. The Barnum show of 1873, with its two rings, was the first large enough to accommodate such a feature.[21] Yet there is nothing to suggest from the route book that it had any type of racing competition.

The idea for Barnum's New Roman Hippodrome must have been his own. In his autobiography he referred to a "long-cherished plan of exhibiting a

---

21. An exception to this took place indoors across the country in San Francisco, where, on the site of the old Mechanics Pavilion, John Wilson's Hippodrome was attracting audiences in 1865. The place was arranged with two rings, an inner and outer one. In the larger, all sorts of races were contested—hurdle, chariot, Roman, pony, and even running. The smaller ring was used for Ella Zoyara's principal act on horseback, for Painter and Dorand's *la perche équipoise*, for exhibition of the trained colt, Othello, and for other gymnastic and acrobatic activities. Several events were featured during the short season. A number of hose companies vied for championship of the mile run around the oval track. And pacing and trotting horse races were offered with purses amounting to $100 and $250. This venture was within a permanent structure and of a short life. The population of California at that time was not of sufficient numbers to support lengthy engagements. The first to use "Hippodrome" in the title of an American circus was Dan Rice in 1852-54, but there was no hippodrome track. Others were Levi J. North, June & Co., and Rufus Welch, 1853; H. C. Lee, 1854. The true originator was Victor Franconi in Paris, copied by Batty in London.

Roman Hippodrome, Zoological Institute, Aquaria, and Museum of unsurpassing extent and magnificence." His propensity for "bigness," for topping his previous achievements, for an enjoyment of public acknowledgment, and, yes, because of the financial success of the 1873 tenting season, all supported the daring of such a scheme. In a letter to Gordon L. Ford, Barnum justified the move in the following manner: "I felt a great *desire* to do a *big thing* for the public & to make it quite unobjectionable to the most refined & moral. I think I have succeeded. It is my last "crowning effort."[22] This, at the age of sixty-three, was to be his final hurrah, elevating, free of all objectionable features and appealing to the patronage of the most moral and refined classes—the ultimate and lasting gemstone to adorn the Barnum public image.

There is no indication how early in 1873 the plans for this last "crowning effort" were set in motion. We know that Barnum had arranged to make a visit to Europe in September to, as he stated in his autobiography, "run over and see the International Exhibition at Vienna."[23] But, whenever, the decision was made

---

22. Barnum, P. T., *Selected Letters*. New York: Columbia University Press, 1983, p. 181.

23. Barnum, P. T., *Struggles and Triumphs*. New York: Alfred A. Knopf, 1927, p. 690. On the other hand, in a letter to Joseph Henry sent from Bridgeport and dated September 19 [Barnum, *Selected Letters*, p. 177], Barnum indicated his European trip was to investigate the possibility of sending a balloon across the Atlantic. He claimed a long-time interest in aerial navigation and was at this time prepared to consult with authorities in England and France and to put up the money for such a flight [New York *Times*, September 18, 1873, p. 5], the bottom line being that a successful project of this nature could show profitable returns by merely exhibiting the

before he left the country.

After attending the Vienna fair and then traveling to Berlin, the news was received from his representatives—W. C. Coup and S. H. Hurd—that the New York and Harlem Railroad Company property at Fourth Avenue and Twenty-sixth Street could be leased. The site was said to be the only vacant grounds in New York City large enough to accommodate the hippodrome Barnum envisioned. It had been rented to various parties after the station was abandoned and the place was deserted with the opening of Grand Central Station at 42$^{nd}$ Street in 1871. Barnum immediately wired back the go-ahead for the property to be secured.

Meanwhile, he was fast at work in Europe. He claims to have visited all the zoological gardens, circuses, and public exhibitions wherever he went—the Hippodrome at Paris, the Circus Renz at Vienna, Myers' Circus at Dresden, Silamonski and Carré's Circus at Cologne, the Zoological Gardens at Hamburg, Amsterdam and other continental cities—thereby acquiring various novelties and valuable ideas. By November 18$^{th}$, he had purchased nearly a "ship load" of birds and animals at Hamburg. He then moved on to England where, on January 2$^{nd}$, he contracted with John and George Sanger to purchase duplicates of the entire wardrobe and paraphernalia connected with the pageant of *The Congress of Monarchs* which had been exhibited at the Agricultural Hall in London, four or five years before. For the sum of £33,000 he received the full list of char-

---

balloon, not to mention the balloonist.

iots, costumes, trappings, flags, banners, etc.—£13,000 to be paid in advance, the remainder at the fulfillment of the terms of the contract.[24] This was confirmed by W. C. Coup in his *Sawdust and Spangles*. He stated that *The Congress of Monarchs* cost "Mr. Barnum and myself" over $40,000.

The managerial staff for the Hippodrome company was much the same as the previous few years of circus operation. P. T. Barnum as the nominal proprietor was assisted by William C. Coup, Dan Castello, and Samuel H. Hurd. Coup was general manager and Castello "director of amusements." Hurd, Barnum's ex-son-in-law, was treasurer and in charge of looking out for Barnum's interests. Charles W. Fuller, a man of wide experience, was the general agent. David S. Thomas was the press agent.

James M. Nixon was acquired to assist Castello. This was a wise choice. Although Castello came into this with some years of experience as an equestrian director, his requisites for developing dramatic spectacle were far inferior to Nixon's. It appears to this writer that, although Barnum supplied the grand scheme for the Roman Hippodrome, Nixon's hand at bringing it off was far more instrumental than he has heretofore been given credit.

The finished Hippodrome was a structure of some 400 by 200 feet (larger than a football field). The covering or canopy above the performing space, eighty feet in width, consisted of light waterproof canvas,

---

24. *Ibid.*, p. 691-696.

manufactured for the purpose in the style of an Italian pavilion, with alternate stripes of rich and variegated colors. Six wooden spars one-hundred feet in height were the main support of the flexible roof—each one, projecting through, was festooned with flags. The track itself was thirty-five feet wide at the ends and twenty-six at the sides, with a total circumference of one-fifth mile.[25]

As one passed through the main entrance on Madison Avenue, the whole length of the right side of the building, beneath the tiered seating, served as the menagerie—penned animals on the right of the passage and cages on the left. On the Twenty-seventh Street corner was a large aquarium. The left side of the structure was occupied as stables for the ring stock.

The family circle, on the Twenty-sixth Street side, was furnished with benches covered by carpeting; the gallery, on the Fourth Avenue side, with plain seating; the parquet, on the Twenty-seventh Street side, with cane-bottom chairs; the orchestra section, extending nearly the full length of one side, with patent iron folding-chairs. Four sumptuous private boxes, accommodating eight people each, were located near the Madison Avenue entrance. On the opposite side were retiring rooms for ladies, "supplied with all the necessary assistants for toilet arrangement."[26]

A large area in the center of the arena, surrounded

---

25. Leslie, Frank, *Frank Leslie's Illustrated Newspaper*, May 9, 1874, p. 139.

26. *Ibid.*

by the hippodrome track, was enclosed with a light railing. A roadway was placed through it, branching at either end into two entrances. On both sides of this were grassy plots supporting an abundance of flowers. At each end of the area was a fountain of running water; and midway there was a music stand. And somewhere was located a pond where "graceful swans disport at ease." Between each post, suspended from the roof, were mechanical birds, made in Paris, which issued forth sweet chirping sounds as the audience was being ushered to their seats.[27] For lighting, there were chandeliers over this enclosure, augmented by two rows of gas lights around the track and seating area. The entrance through which the various processions and chariots entered to the scene of action, located at the easterly, or Fourth Avenue end of the interior, was thirty feet high and twenty feet wide.

On April 27th, as banners waved their welcome atop the canvas roof, the opening night patrons crowded their way into the huge structure to bear witness to this gala event; but they would not celebrate the presence of the star attraction—Barnum was still at sea, a few days shy of New York harbor.

The commentary in the New York *Herald* suggested that 15,000 New Yorkers created a crush never before seen at any public place of amusement in the city since the days of Ellen Tree or Fanny Ellsler at the old Park Theatre. The jam was so great, it stated, that the police were almost powerless—although at times exercised

---
27. *Ibid.*

their clubs vigorously upon the hats and heads of the surging crowd—and a number of ladies fainted under the pressure of the pushing and shoving multitude.[28]

From newspaper accounts of the evening, we learn that the program opened with a brilliant pageant minutes in length, and bearing no relationship to the rest of the program. It took the place of the old-fashioned *grand entrée*. The long procession around the hippodrome track consisted of magnificent chariots and *tableaux* cars and long lines of court retainers and solders, mounted and on foot, in which many of the courts of Europe and the East were represented. The theme reflected a nineteenth century passion for world discovery—a curiosity about not only ancient cultures but of existing ones as well.

There is no doubt this spectacle was breathtaking to an 1874 audience or that it was the most luxurious show of pageantry ever attempted on this continent. It was repeatedly described by observers in such phrases as "huge gilded cars," "gorgeously mounted chariots," "splendidly caparisoned camels, elephants, horses, and ponies," and "hundreds of performers in elegant costumes." The elaborate procession would draw awestruck attention from audience and press during its New York run and, in the future, wherever the show was presented.

The *grand entrée* was supervened by a series of races and variety performances. There was flat racing

---

28. Loeffler, Robert James, "A Re-Examination of the History of Madison Square Garden," Part One, in *Bandwagon*, March-April, 1973, p. 8.

between men mounted on English thoroughbreds; racing between men standing astride two horses; Roman two-horse chariots racing; English jockey racing; hurdle racing and, let us not fail to mention, elephant, monkey, and ostrich racing. There was also a liberty race between some twenty horses without riders or harness. At the end of each of the races, the victor was handed a flag and then made a circle around the course to receive the approbation of the audience.

In between the races there were various specialty acts. They were introduced to the arena in an elegant *barouche* with a coachman and footman in livery and driven once around before performing. There was Mons. Loyal and Millson & Lazelle on a trapeze, Mons. Joignerey exhibiting feats of strength, and Signor Leonchi dressed as an Indian, demonstrating his skill with a lasso while mounted on horseback. A bit of satirical fun was offered when "Mme. Pompadour's Carriage in Central Park" was represented by a double turnout carrying a dozen dignified monkeys. There was also a comical race between a half-dozen such primates mounted on ponies. The program terminated with a female charioteer racing four horses abreast against a male counterpart.

April 30th marked the arrival from Liverpool of P. T. Barnum on the steamer *Scotia*. That night he attended his great dream for the first time. Once the audience became aware of his presence, they were energetic in calling him out. He then stepped into the *barouche* and, standing hat in hand, was driven around the arena to cheers of welcome and resounding applause. He termed that night "the greatest assemblage of people ever gathered in one building in New York." And added that his "enthusiastic reception was at once a testimonial of the public appreciation of one of [his] greatest efforts in [his] managerial career, and a verdict that it was a complete and gratifying success."[29]

After only a few weeks into the run, novelties were being added to the program. A sequence with Leonchi's Tribe of Indians and Mexican Rangers depicted various scenes of Indian life—preparing a camp on the plains, a buffalo hunt by six young chiefs, a Canadian snowshoe race, a hurdle race by six young braves on their ponies, a hurdle footrace by twelve young men, a man racing against a horse, etc.

Added to the non-riding acts were Satsuma and Little All Right, who performed their Japanese ladder balancing act. Charles White entered a den of performing lions as the big cage was pulled around the oval by a four-horse team to allow vantage from the whole of the arena. Mlle. Victoria, whose last name is unknown to us, walked the wire and eventually crossed it on a velocipede.

In mid-July a satirical sequence called *Donnybrook Fair; or, The Lancaster Races* was added. The publicity explained it as "twenty minutes of drollery and rollicking fun interspersed with comical situations, ludicrous scenes and life-like portraits." This appears to be a series of clown acts still in keeping

---
29. Barnum, *Struggles and Triumphs*, p. 698.

with the nature of the hippodromic program. Events included a greased pole competition, wheelbarrow, sack, and donkey races, and a sketch about the trading of horses. There were burlesque fist fights and *mêlées* midst the wildest confusion, as the women urged on their favorite Irish fighters.[30] All this was a seeming burlesque, using a nineteenth-century view of the Irish character. Attached to this was a segment—the Lancaster Races—that included an English steeplechase.

Beginning Friday, June 26th, and continuing to the following Friday, the regular performances were supplemented by amateur athletic contests, with prizes announced to be bestowed to the winners. Contestants were restricted to men who had never performed for hire or had never been compensated for teaching the feat in which there were said to excel. The competitions included pole-vaulting, rope-climbing, tossing the caber (a roughly trimmed tree trunk used in Scottish sports), standing long jump, *battoute* leaping, weight lifting, pole-climbing, a bayonet exercise, shot put, wrestling, high jump, foot boxing, hop-skip-and-jump, dumbbells, walking, and various footraces.[31]

---

30. Barnum, P. T., "Advance Courier," 1875, p. 20. This edition, which is used as a source for this publication, is believed to be almost identical to the one issued in 1874.

31. New York *Clipper*, July 4, 1874, p. 11; July 11, 1874, p. 115. As noted in the *Clipper*, the contests were scheduled as follows: Friday, June 26th: pole-vaulting; rope-climbing; mile race. Saturday, June 27th: wheelbarrow race; tossing the caber; relief race; one-mile handicap race; standing long jump; one hundred yard dash; half-mile handicap. Monday, June 29th: boy's race for under sixteen years of age, battoute leaping; rope-climbing; half-mile walk; hand or health life; half-mile run; pole race; shot put; three-

At the beginning of July it was announced that Barnum had arranged for twelve experimental balloon ascensions. For some time he had entertained an interest in navigational flight and more recently contemplated the launching of a transcontinental balloon from New York City, piloted by three aeronauts of different nationalities, for which he was prepared to expend any sum necessary to accomplish. Money was to be no object.[32]

Balloon navigation was an intriguing notion in the public mind. And there is no doubt that Barnum was serious about these experiments and fully intended to make a Barnum-like effort to conquer the problems of an Atlantic crossing. But it was also a shrewd move on his part to combine scientific study with show business rewards. As it turned out, Prof. Washington Donaldson's lifts into space were remarkably instrumental in attracting audiences to the Hippodrome; and, indeed, became a feature nearly as important as the show inside the tent.

On July 7th, the day set for the first ascension, the balloon was carefully inflated during the matinee performance, presumably on the infield of the

---

legged race; 220 yards race; heavy hammer throw; wrestling; professional one-mile walk. Wednesday, July 1st: running high jump; wrestling, second trial; one-mile race; running long jump; hurdle race; 1/8 mile, eight hurdles three-feet high. Thursday, July 2nd: quarter-mile race, la savate; foot boxing or a French style of self-defense, amateur one-mile walk; hop-skip-and-jump; heavy single dumbbell; putting 100 pound dumbbell from shoulder; wrestling, final trial; hurdle race, 100 yards, four hurdles three-feet high.

32. New York *Times*, September 18, 1874, p. 5.

Hippodrome. But, alas, once filled, it was discovered there was insufficient lifting power to allow a proper ascent to be made. So the following day the balloon was emptied and refilled with gas from another company, but not in time for the scheduled lift-off. Successful voyages occurred, however, on the following two days.

An effort was made to bolster attendance for the final two weeks of the season. Prices were lowered, allowing all events to be witnessed for only 50¢. In addition, since professional pedestrianism was experiencing a decade of popularity at this time, it was announced that Edward Mullen, a well known pedestrian, would attempt to walk around the Hippodrome oval for a distance of 500 miles within a six-day period. For this the box office would be open day and night, price 50¢.

Mullen's scheduled start was set at 12:05 a.m., July 20th. An oval shaped track was positioned within the hippodrome course as an inner ring. This allowed for the walk to occur continually throughout the regular hippodromic program without interruption of any event. Representatives of the Committee of Arrangements were present at the site day and night to certify complete compliance with the rules of pedestrianism. Unfortunately, Mullen was forced to abandon the effort after the matinee on the 23rd because of swelling in one of his legs. He had sprained a tendon at an exhibition of his skills some two weeks earlier, from which, as he discovered, he had not fully recovered.

On Friday, July 24th, Prof. Donaldson made what was advertised as a first "Grand Press Ascension" in the completed large balloon, *P. T. Barnum*, expressly constructed for experimental flight, to ascertain the existence of an easterly current. The craft was made of the best materials and under the supervision of Donaldson himself. The gas bag supported a strong but light wicker basket, eight feet long, five feet wide, and four feet high, large enough to accommodate six or more people, including reporters, and provisions for two days of airborne adventure, still leaving space for ballast, scientific instruments, and other necessities. The practice of balloon excursions for newspaper people would, within a year, end in disaster.

The inflation began at 8:00 a.m. and the ascent occurred at 4:15 p.m., just five minutes following the finish of the matinee. Accompanied by five or six representatives of the local press, the Professor and his flying machine arose from the Hippodrome infield and disappeared through an opening in the canvas roof. The large crowd which had gathered outside the building greeted the passengers with cheers of approval. Donaldson, posed heroically, hat in hand, acknowledged the waving mass below. The balloon drifted, not east, but rapidly northward and within a matter of fifteen minutes or so was out of sight.

The Hippodrome season closed on August 1st. The only novelty for the week was another pedestrian event. C. N. Payne "accepting Mr. Barnum's proffer for the free use of the walking course inside the inner enclosure of the Hippodrome," as the advertisement stated it, appeared on Wednesday, July 29th.[33] At 9 o'clock that evening he commenced the feat of walking 115 miles in less than twenty-four hours. Starting off with his best time, he made the first mile in ten minutes and twenty seconds. But, in the end, he failed to meet his goal; for at 9:04 p.m. on Thursday, exactly twenty-four hours from his starting time, he had traversed only sixty-seven and a half miles.

Following the Saturday performance, the obstinate ostriches were rounded up, all the trappings and costumes were packed, and the whole of the arenic spectacle loaded up and conveyed to Boston, where Barnum's Great Roman Hippodrome opened under canvas just two days later.

---

33. *Ibid.*, July 27, 1874, p. 7.

# THE RECYCLING OF THE DAN RICE PARIS PAVILION CIRCUS

Dan Rice's Paris Pavilion Circus opened at the Richmond Market lot in Baltimore on November 13, 1871. The show was certainly the most extravagant of its kind to ever visit the city. The initial plan was, after a successful winter season, to take the outfit to Europe for the year of 1872. A large frame building was erected, the interior of which was decorated with flowers, fountains, and thousands of gas jets. The dress circle, parquet, and boxes were adorned with expensive imported velvet carpets and furnished with elegant cane-bottomed chairs and comfortable settees. The entire amphitheatre appeared to be much too costly for a prudent investment. But wait. It was not originally assembled and constructed for the Baltimore winter season.

Five years earlier a scheme had been devised to send a circus company to the Paris Exposition of 1867. The investors were the "Flatfoots"—Avery Smith, Gerard C. Quick, and John J. Nathans—joined by Dr. Gilbert R. Spalding and David Bidwell. The partnership chartered the large steamer, *Guiding Star*, to convey the company, horses, ponies, mules, a performing buffalo, wardrobe, trappings, and the portable amphitheatre, which was to be put together in sections on an open space near the exposition grounds in Paris. W. T. B. Van Orden was sent in advance to prepare the way.

The amphitheatre, wooden with a canvas top, was made by a Mr. Kennedy of Albany, New York. It was 118 feet in diameter, with forty outside panels, each eight-feet wide and sixteen-feet high. They were fitted together by hinges between sturdy posts one foot in width which interlocked with the flooring, making the pavilion as substantial as an ordinary frame structure. Masts around the outside were arranged to bear the colors of each nation and the private boxes within were designed to be ornamented with damask draperies in like manner.

The interior housed a forty-two foot ring and seating to accommodate somewhere around 2,000 spectators, not counting the standing room. A splendidly furnished box over the main entrance was reserved expressly for the French Emperor and his royal family; another was arranged for the orchestra on the opposite side of the ring, over the passageway to the dressing area. The parquet, which was nearest the ring, was furnished with cane-bottomed settees. John C. Kunzog, in his biography of Rice, has this area seating 540 people; the *Clipper* gives a figure of 760. Directly behind this were forty-four private boxes, excluding the imperial loge, divided by a walnut railing and each fitted with six cane-bottomed easy chairs. The balcony or family circle seated over 1,000 on three-person, carpet-covered, folding benches. The ring, encompassed by a two-foot high wall, and the aisle to the dressing rooms were the only spaces without wooden flooring.

A more detailed description has been given in Kunzog's biography. There was red carpeting on the floor, lace curtains covering the wall openings, and heavy draperies serving as an acoustical aid. Brass fixtures on the lobby wall held velvet-covered ropes that served as handrails. Tricolor velvet curtains hung over the entrance to the dressing rooms. Above the ring, extending from center pole to sidewalls, were velvet-covered ropes from which hung the flags of all nations. Around the lobby in front were fountains depicting birds and children in pools of water. Baskets of flowers hung on the walls. About the building, some one thousand open-flame jets flickered from elegant chandeliers. A Drummond light hanging from the center pole gave out bright illumination during the performance.[34]

There were "withdrawing rooms" for both men and women situated above the performer's entry at the end of the lobby. These were furnished with washbowls fitted with running water and supplied with soap and towel racks. Near each rack hung a device that gave off a spray of perfumed powder each time a towel was used. The toilets were curtained off for privacy. They resembled a large funnel with a wooden seat. The overflow water from the fountains was piped to

---

34. Kunzog, John C., *The One-Horse Show*, self-published 1962, pp. 269-277. He used no citations in his text.

them, creating a continuous stream which was flushed into the municipal sewer, preventing the escape of disagreeable gas and odor. In the entrance lobby were three ticket windows for the expeditious handling of patrons, while directly opposite was the refectory stall that offered candy, fruits, popcorn, peanuts, cookies and lemonade.[35]

An exemplary group of performers was assembled under the title of American Championship Circus. It included James Robinson, champion bareback rider, and his son, Clarence; equestrian Frank Pastor, brother of the famous Tony Pastor; Robert Stickney of the respected Stickney family; champion leaper, George M. Kelly; French-and-Spanish clown, Lorenzo Mayo; rider and tumbler, Charles Rivers; and many other attractions. The equestrian manager was David Bidwell.

It might be noted that the display of any flag other than the French colors was prohibited at this time. According to John A. Dingess, Frank Pastor, who used three large flags in his act, was the first to unfold the stars and stripes at a French circus. This bravado was witnessed by Napoleon and the Empress. It was also here that Edwin Derious was gored by a buffalo, stricken with paralysis, and disabled for ten years prior to his death.

After arriving in Paris, and when nearly all the preparations for their opening had been completed, vehement opposition by local managers influenced

---

35. *Ibid.*

the evocation of a local law that prevented the erection of any wooden building within the city limits. Consequently, the circus proprietors could assemble their pavilion, but instead arranged to perform at the *Théâtre Prince Impériale*, on the *Rue du Temps*. The show remained there for six months before removing to the Holborn Amphitheatre, London, for another three months. The unused pavilion together with its equipment was returned to the United States and stored in New Orleans.[36]

It is quite probable that the "Flatfoot" shares of this unused amphitheatre were purchased by Spalding and Bidwell, for in 1870 the pavilion was resurrected in New Orleans on the corner of Canal and Villere Streets to house entertainments for the summer season. One can speculate that a motive for removing this white elephant from storage and displaying it at this time and place was for a possible sale.

The Paris Circus Pavilion was opened on Easter Sunday, April 17th, with C. W. Noyes' Crescent City Circus. The New Orleans *Daily Picayune* suggested that the entertainment at this new place of amusement was well attended on opening night. "The like of such

---

36. Dingess, John, manuscript, p. 270. Kunzog's version is somewhat different: "The show played a year in France, but business was not up to expectations. The American offerings were a surfeit in Europe, while blackface minstrelsy failed to appeal to French people. From Paris the circus moved to London where Bidwell fell ill. Rather than trust the venture to inexperienced hands, Bidwell and the American Champion Circus bid farewell to Europe and returned to New Orleans less than eighteen months after embarking on the quest for the pot of gold at the end of the European rainbow." Kunzog, *op. cit.*, p. 272.

a place has long been wished for in New Orleans, and our play going public cannot but appreciate the efforts of the management to please them. The performance, too, is excellent. Mr. Noyes has supplied his Crescent City Circus with every possible attraction."[37]

The roster included the Wilson Brothers, gymnasts; and riders Fred Barclay, Mrs. Noyes, and star performer Wooda Cook. Sharing the billing was aerialist Millie Turnour. Miss Turnour's daring act was detailed at this time in the *Daily Picayune*:

> "A swinging bar is suspended about 50 feet in the air. Upon this simple bar she balances, swings, suspends and enacts feats which are equally the amazement, the admiration and the fear of all who behold her. Her turns in the air are marvelous to behold, and as she descends to the stage, head downwards on a single rope without the assistance of her hands, the tumultuous applause which invariably greets her, is an involuntary tribute to so much courage united with so much grace."[38]

Performances were given nightly, with 1:00 p.m. matinees on Mondays, Thursdays, and Saturdays. Private boxes with six chairs, $5.00; private boxes with three chairs, $3.00; boxes with a single chair, $1.00; dress circle chair, 75¢; family circle chair, 50¢; dress

---

37. New Orleans *Daily Picayune*, April 19, 1870, p. 1.

38. *Ibid.*, April 29, 1870, p. 2.

circle chair (colored), $1.00; family circle chair (colored), 50¢. Matinees were slightly less.

For the closing week of May 2nd there was a change in the program. The spectacle *Sprites of the Silver Shower* was offered, as was the grand tournament, *Field of the Cloth of Gold*. On Tuesday, Mrs. Noyes took a benefit. The *Daily Picayune* reported that "she showed to great advantage the perfect power and mastery she has over her spirited Arab horse, D'Talma, and executed some feats which drew forth repeated and deserved applause."[39] Wooda Cook took a benefit on Thursday and Charles Noyes on the closing Saturday, May 7th.

With the circus gone, the pavilion stood vacant until Monday, May 16th.

On the evening of this date the Berger Family of bell ringers, who had been performing at the Academy of Music, took a benefit "tendered by the citizens of New Orleans." On the 24th, the first of a series of ads appeared in the *Daily Picayune*, offering to rent the Paris Circus Pavilion "by the day or night, for balls, picnics, and any first-class entertainment."[40] The ads continued until mid-July, then disappeared. One can speculate that the Spalding and Bidwell pavilion was dismantled around this time.

It was announced in the *Clipper* in the spring of 1871 that the Paris Pavilion had been acquired by Dan Rice, who had arrived in New Orleans on January 7, 1871, on his own boat after a lengthy and prosperous tour.[41]

39. *Ibid.*, May 4, 1870, p. 1.
40. *Ibid.*, May 24, 1870, p. 10.
41. New York *Clipper*, March 25, 1871, p. 407. C. G. Sturtevant stated in

Spalding and Bidwell had found themselves a buyer.

The price Rice paid is not known. According to Kunzog, it varied from $200,000 to twice that sum (an estimate that appears to be much too high). In addition to the building, the deal included a plant used to manufacture gas for illumination, the Apollonicon bandwagon, hundreds of costumes, carriages and wagons, saddles and other appurtenances, but no animals. Since Rice did not pay for all of this in full, but gave notes for the balance, Spalding insisted that his son, Harry W. Spalding, be hired as manager as a way of keeping a check on the finances of the show.[42]

The opulent arena was transported to St. Louis and there erected at Sixth and Washington Avenues, on the property where the old Lindell Hotel had stood. It was announced in the *Missouri Democrat* on April 4th, two weeks before opening, that the pavilion was "fast approaching completion."[43] This brings us to an issue basic to our investigation. Given the complexity and unwieldy nature of the full pavilion, what was the extent of time, labor, and expense needed to tear down and set up? More on this later.

The Dan Rice's Paris Pavilion Circus opened for business in St. Louis on April 17, 1871, exactly one year from the day the structure had made its debut in

---

"Little Biographies of Famous American Circus Men," Number 9, *White Tops*, October, 1928, p. 8, that Dan Rice purchased the Paris Pavilion outfit in 1870.

42. New York *Clipper*, March 25, 1871, p. 273.

43. St. Louis *Missouri Democrat*, April 4, 1871, p. 4.

New Orleans. But there was a "fly in the ointment." Just a few blocks away, pitched on the Lindell lot at the corner of Washington and Eleventh Avenues, was Robinson's Combination Menagerie, Aviary and Circus. It, too, opened on the 17th and, according to the *Missouri Democrat* of the following day, opened to standing room. And, in spite of the competition from Rice, it continued to do well throughout the one-week engagement. The advantage was, of course, the additional bird and animal exhibits—not to mention the featured riding, leaping, and tumbling by the "Apollo Belvidere of the Arena," Robert Stickney, Sr.

Credit the congenial people of St. Louis; the Paris Pavilion Circus was playing to good business as well. They came to enjoy the comfort of the interior accommodations and the outstanding ring performance. Rice carried no menagerie or sideshow, no lemonade and peanut peddlers, and no street procession other than the Apollonicon bandwagon.

The program consisted of such spectacle pieces as "The Court of Isabella, Ex-Queen of Spain, in an Equestrian Social," along with the usual equestrian, acrobatic, and gymnastic feats. Prof. Nelson tossed his two children about like Indian-rubber. "They pirouette while standing on the soles of their father's feet, and wear a smile of confidence, and perform with the grace and activity of a Bonfanti. They give acrobatic acts that would be credited to matured and skillful gymnasts." The great *battoute* leaper, Fred O'Brien, easily cleared four horses upon which tour men stood. "The performance produced a chilling effect, and the applause was immense." There was William Morgan's daring hurdle riding. The bareback pirouette, and somersault riding of Fred Barclay was justly admired. "He is, moreover, an actor of no mean ability, as was manifested by his impersonation of a Comanche warrior." This portrayal was part of an enactment of the sports and pastimes of the Comanche tribe, including a buffalo hunt, called "Life Pictures on the Prairies." Add to this Rice's milk-white Arabian charger, Stephen A. Douglas, and his eighteen-year-old blind talking horse, Excelsior, Jr., "who seemed to understand every word addressed to him and instantly obeyed every command."[44]

It was Rice's practice with the multi-day stands to introduce new acts during the run. Miss Lizzie Marcellus, "juvenile queen of the *manege*," was brought forth as the bareback equestrienne. She had been apprenticed to Rice from about 1866. The Victorelli Brothers worked an act entitled "The School of Physical Education." The Cylocephalus, or monkey-man, made an appearance. And the heralded bareback rider, Master Wooda Cook, made his debut on the 26th. He was a back-and-forward somersault rider, billed as turning twenty-four consecutive somersaults on a swiftly running horse.

There was also the "two-woman" trapeze act, Lila and Zoe. Zoe, blindfolded and encased in a sack, swung from a trapeze, turned a somersault in mid-air, and ended by clutching a single rope, a version of *l'echelle*

---

44. *Ibid.*, April 19, 20, 21, 22, 1871, pp. 4.

*perileuse*. It has been said that their leap-and-catch performance may have represented the first appearance of a female catcher.

Others in the company included youthful rider Master Dick Clark, the French equestrienne, Mme. Richmonde; the Chilian grymnast Adolph Gonzales; the Siegrist family and Antonio Brothers; Mike Austin on the horizontal bars; and John Callan, strong-man.

The show had four clowns in addition to Rice. Lorenzo Mayo was a French-and-Spanish clown, said to have escaped the siege of Paris in a balloon. August Siegrist doubled as a German dialect clown. Edward Hailey was described as an American colloquial clown. William G. Miles, the "Equestrian Joe Jefferson," performed as a comic actor and acrobat. Mayo and Siegrist were the only ones of the group of any note. Indeed, during the tour one journalist remarked: "Dan Rice's clowns, in their efforts to be funny, remind one of the attempts of a very small, juvenile duck to swallow an exceedingly large frog—ignominious failures."[45] Perhaps more laugh provoking were Rice's trick mules, Pete and Barney. O'Brien, Callan, Clark, Miles, and Bailey had been with Rice the previous year, successfully touring the river towns on the steamboat *Will S. Hays*.

And, of course, there was Rice himself. Throughout the tour he was well-behaved, there being no indication of impropriety or of missed performances. His

---

45. Jackson (Michigan) *Daily Citizen*, June 5, 1871, p. 4. By late July newspaper ads revealed that wire-walker Monsieur DeLave and the gymnast Antonio Brothers were on the bill. The Nelson family had disappeared.

ring appearances included familiar discourses of fun and philosophy. His drawing power was still apparent, the question regarding his loyalty to the Union during the Civil War having, either through forgiveness or forgetfulness by the public, no negative after-effect. The single, disapproving commentary came from the Mobile *Daily Register*, which noted displeasure with his political dialogues. He is "too much in the habit of talking politics or making political hits in the ring," the scribe observed, "a thing, by the way, no matter who the person the joke is upon, or the section of the country referred to, is out of place. No one knows better than Col. Rice himself, a shrewd and veteran circus manager, that the people understand how to take such allusions, and have very little or no belief in the political faith of 'show people'."[46] But Col. Dan was still the greatest star the American circus had produced to this point in history; so, needless to mention, throughout the tour Rice and the elegant pavilion were the main attractions. Quite ironically, however, it was this very year that an even greater name was being connected with circusdom, one that would far outlast Rice's fame—P. T. Barnum.

The record of the Rice itinerary for 1871 is incomplete. We know he was billed to open a two-week Chicago stand on Monday night, May 15th; but we don't know his whereabouts between that date and the St. Louis closing, with the exception of Kankakee, Illinois, on May 12th. There are similar lapses of infor-

---

46. Mobile *Daily Register*, January 25, 1872, p. 1.

mation on his wanderings throughout the season.

The Chicago *Times* reported that Alderman McCaffrey had offered a resolution during recent common council proceedings that Rice should be prohibited from showing within the city limits until he complied with an ordinance that required him to take out a license. Apparently he paid the fee, because the performance went on as scheduled.

The pavilion, which the *Tribune* assessed as "a perfect marvel, being fully equal to a first-class theatre in all respects," was erected in Lake Park on Michigan Avenue between Randolph and Washington Streets. The leapers, led by Fred O'Brien, were particularly noteworthy, the writer felt. He was also impressed with the trained horses, Douglas and Excelsior; Prof. Nelson and his two children "who altogether surpassed anything of the kind which has been presented in Chicago;" the extraordinary tumbling of Gonzales; and the hurdle riding of William Morgan. We might add, he was also appreciative of the elegantly fitted private box—the one that had been arranged for the French Emperor in 1867—at the disposal of members of the Chicago press.[47] The Chicago *Times* reported the entertainment "to be upon a scale of excellence fully commensurate with the beauty of the structure in which it was given."[48] On the 17th the trapezists, Lila and Zoe, were introduced to Chicago audiences. On the morning of Friday, the 26th at 10:00 a.m., a complimen-

---

47. Chicago *Tribune*, May 16, 1871, p. 5.

48. Chicago *Times*, May 16, 1871, p. 2.

tary benefit was given in aid of the Chicago Orphan Asylum. The run ended the following day.

The company went from Chicago into Michigan. There were a series of one-day stands before setting up in Detroit on the corner of Michigan Avenue and Fourth Street for four days. This city hosted more than its share of visiting circuses in the months of May and June. Before Rice, James Robinson's Champion Circus had appeared on May 12th and 13th, followed closely by VanAmburgh's Golden Menagerie on May 26th and 27th. Then, when Rice left town, L. B. Lent's New York Circus moved in for June 12th and 13th.

The Detroit *Free Press* revealed that Rice's first day's program on June 8th opened with the grand entry of "The Court of Isabella, ex-Queen of Spain, in an Equestrian School." This was followed by the *battoute* leaping of Frederick O'Brien; Dan Rice and his educated horse Stephen A. Douglas; Prof. Nelson and his two boys; the aerial stunts of Lila and Zoe; William H. Morgan's bareback riding; and finished with the comic antics of the mules, Pete and Barney. If the paper's list is complete, one can see there were only six acts following the grand entry, far fewer than within the usual circus program. Where were Wooda Cook, Lizzie Marcellus, Fred Barclay, and others? Were they saved for later in the run? We know Rice changed the program on particular days, with new acts appearing as an encouragement for repeat patronage. For example, on the 10th a spectacle called "Sports and Pastimes of the Celestials" was introduced, consisting of a number of acrobats and gymnasts forming living pyramids and other tests in keeping with the Oriental theme.

The newspaper repeated the praises of the earlier stands and the usual assessment of good houses. "An immense business was done yesterday [June 8th], and all in attendance were unanimously of the opinion that no better arena exhibition was ever given in Detroit."[49] Particularly impressive was the sack and blindfold act of Zoe, of which "no more desperate and startling feat has ever been undertaken," and the tight-rope performances of Mons. DeLave (a new acquisition since St. Louis) and August Siegrist.[50] On the 10th, the last day in Detroit, the children, matrons, and officers of the Protestant Orphan Asylum were invited to the matinee.

According to the Jackson, Michigan *Daily Citizen*, in referring to a June 3rd stand in that city, there was a side show attached to the circus which exhibited the "Life of Christ." This had to be a scavenger outfit, independent of Rice's troupe, taking advantage of the crowds on circus day. There was certainly nothing of the like allowed on the lot. As one newspaper affirmed: "No humbug sideshows are permitted on the grounds, and the audience will be nourished with a plentiful supply of ice water."[51]

There were surprisingly few multi-day dates. I have found none during its tour of Ohio, but when the company entered New York state in early July there

---

49. Detroit *Free Press*, June 9, 1871, p. 1.

50. *Ibid.*, June 10, 1871, p. 1.

51. *Ibid.*, June 7, 1871, p. 1.

were three and four-day stands in Buffalo, Rochester, Syracuse, Troy, and Albany. Here they had to share the territory with L. B. Lent's New York Circus, Sluthour & Son's Great Continental, the Great Commonwealth, Howes' Great London, the Great Eastern, and P. T. Barnum's Great Traveling Menagerie, Caravan and Hippodrome. There were many occasions when a circus had just preceded them or was advertising in advance to follow them in. And half of their competitors had menageries.

A four-day stand in Buffalo, July $5^{th}$-$8^{th}$, on the corner of Main and Virginia Streets was one of the first New York dates for Rice. "Nothing to offend the most fastidious will be permitted." For those who wanted to avoid the rush at the box office, tickets were available at the music store of Messrs. Cottier & Denton.

Rice felt competition from Howes' Great London, exhibiting in the United States for the first time and equipped with the finest street procession of any show, which followed on the $13^{th}$ and $14^{th}$, but was being advertised as early as the $6^{th}$, "Wait for Howes' Great London Menagerie and Circus, Both Exhibited Under One Enormous Field Marquee."[52] As if that were not enough, Rice's opening competed with a lingering Fourth of July celebration in downtown Buffalo, but still nearly filled the amphitheatre. "A large portion of these were composed of a class of our citizens whom it is safe to say witnessed a circus exhibition for the first

---

52. Buffalo *Daily Courier*, July 6, 1871, p. 2.

time in their lives."⁵³ In making an observation about the editorial box, a local writer commented, "That any facility should be afforded to scribbling bohemians will be a surprise even to our permanent theatres." And, as to the entertainment, it was considered "so far superior to anything of the kind ever before seen in Buffalo."⁵⁴

On Friday, the 7th, Rice offered a special 10:00 a.m. show. The gross receipts were given to aid the local Society for the Prevention of Cruelty to Animals, a gesture that today might be looked upon as a monumental irony. As a novelty for the children at this performance, Rice introduced into the ring a number of Shetland ponies, the smallest of which was said to weigh thirty pounds.

The Pavilion was erected on Falls Field in Rochester for performances on July 17th through 20th. Advance tickets were available at Dewey's and Reynolds' Arcade. The *Evening Express* reported the pavilion "well-filled" for the opening day afternoon and evening performances. "In fact," it read, "we have never seen a more respectable or better behaved audience at any entertainment of the kind that has ever been given in our city." The performance was also stated a being "superior." "The equestrian feats, somersaults, gymnastic efforts, etc., etc., all possess a freshness and excellence that is worthy of the highest degree of praise."⁵⁵

On the evening of Thursday the 17th the company celebrated the wedding of popular acrobat, C. W.

---

53. *Ibid.*

54. *Ibid.*

55. Rochester *Evening Express*, July 18, 1871, p. 2.

Antonio, to Miss Lottie Harris of Fox's American Theatre, Philadelphia. The post-ceremonial activities, which took place at the Fayette House, included dinner, the presentation of gifts, and a number of speeches, songs, and toasts

On the 18th a strong wind was blowing during the trapeze act of August Siegrist. When he sprang from his pedestal to the catcher he failed to clasp the outstretched hands and fell some forty feet, missing the safety net and striking with his shoulder on the ground. After being assisted to a dressing room, it was ascertained that the injury was not serious. But for the rest of the Rochester engagement at least, the Nelson child, not yet eight years of age, replaced Auguste in the "Leap for Life," a performance perhaps not as deftly rendered but somewhat more thrilling because of the precocity of the callow artist.

A few days later a vague newspaper comment read: "Dan has no female trapeze performers. One of the girls was discovered to be a boy recently, and the other one left and went into Canada."[56] So much for Lila and Zoe. Rice then played Syracuse for the dates of July 26th, 27th, and 28th.

The August 21st opening in Albany was welcomed by a downpour of rain. What would normally have been unpleasantly damp within the amphitheatre did not occur in this instance. In the first place, the structure had been erected prior to the storm. And, of course, with wooden flooring and sides and every-

---

56. Utica *Daily Observer*, August 1, 1871, p. 3.

thing else being carefully sealed, the interior comfort was designed to remain unchanged in any kind of foul weather. The *Argus* reported the accommodations to be the most complete ever presented by any traveling company. "There is no doubt," it stated, "that this pavilion will attract a better class of people than usually attends a circus performance."[57]

The four-day stand was, however, encumbered by opposition from P. T. Barnum's immense organization, which day-and-dated on the 22$^{nd}$ and 23$^{rd}$. Like Rice's, the Barnum outfit had met with rain in Troy on the 21$^{st}$, prior to its Albany arrival. This was Barnum's first year as a circus proprietor and one, thanks to his partners, W. C. Coup and Dan Castello, that proved a great success. The museum was a tremendous feature, the menagerie was well-stocked, and the street procession was impressive. During the season the crowds that flocked to the show necessitated an enlargement of the canvas amphitheatre and an addition of a third daily performance at most places. In Albany two shows were given on the first day and three on the second.

The competition between the two great circuses proved to be a draw, with both doing good business. In addition to creature comforts, Rice had the advantage of location, set up as he was in the heart of the city, while the site for the Barnum people was near the outskirts. This compensated for the disparity in size and flash between the two. Referring to the performance at the Paris Pavilion of the 22$^{nd}$, the *Argus*

---

57. Albany *Argus*, August 22, 1871, p. 4.

man wrote, "The vast amphitheatre was filled from parquet to the most extreme standing aisles of the family circle." And of the Barnum show, "nearly eight thousand people, from every walk in life, attended the afternoon performance, and in the evening the rush was almost overwhelming."[58] It was summarized in the *Argus* of the 24th with, "Ordinarily two arenic exhibitions in Albany at the same time would have proved fatal to both. In this case neither Dan Rice nor Barnum [was] bankrupt, and both will leave with exchequers in a healthy condition."[59]

It might be added here that following the closing performance, Rice's circus band serenaded the Leland brothers, hosts of the Delavan House. When the short concert ended Charley Leland invited the participants and the press to partake of refreshments. The jovial Rice was placed at the head of the table, from where he kept the party alive with anecdotal banter until long after midnight.

A stand in Brooklyn began on September 4th. The New York *Times* read: "Mr. Rice's circus is fitted up in admirable style, and his company is very strong in talent and in numbers."[60] The *Herald* added: "The audience seemed composed of a different class than ordinarily found in a circus, the natural result of Dan Rice's 'new departure' from a traveling lumber yard

---

58. *Ibid.*, August 23, 1871, p. 4.

59. *Ibid.*, August 24, 1871, p. 4. On the 24th the bareback equestrienne, Cordelia, made her first appearance with the show.

60. New York *Times*, September 6, 1871, p. 5.

to an opera house."⁶¹ The engagement was successful the first week, but the second yielded only half houses, rain and apparent disinterest being the cause.

From Brooklyn, Rice went into New Jersey for a few dates, probably to allow the pavilion to be transferred to New York City. At Newark on September 20th and 21st the circus was performed in the Rink. During a showing on opening day the buffalo used in "Life Pictures on the Prairies" decided to step out of character and mingle with the audience. The animal was soon rounded up, its progress being inhibited by the slippery footing of the wooden floor, but not before giving the large assemblage a bit of a scare. From Newark the show moved on to Elizabeth.

The show opened in New York "until further notice," as the advertising phrased it, on September 25th at a 14th Street lot between Second and Third Avenues. There were only two matinees given each week, those being on Wednesdays and Saturdays. The *Times* writer was pleased with both the performance and the ambiance. It was suggested that the latter alone made it worth a visit but the "talent of the artists, and the variety of the programme they interpret[ed]," made the "brightness and comfort" of the place a matter of secondary importance. The conclusion was: "The Paris Pavilion Circus is worthy, in all respects, of its reputation, and we are glad to see that this is increasing by the prestige of a very successful season in the city."⁶² The represen-

---

61. New York *Herald*, September 5, 1871, p. 10.

62. New York *Times*, September 27, 1871, p. 5.

tative from the New York *Clipper* was also impressed, writing, "It is certainly the most comfortable establishment of the kind ever seen in this city."[63] The indefinite run ended, however, after two weeks.

Baltimore was the final stand for the luxurious wood-and-canvas pavilion. It was opened on the Garden Street lot near the Richmond market to a near full house. In the family circle every seat was taken with but few empty seats noticeable in the parquet and boxes, and spectators were standing around the rear of the amphitheatre. "The editorial box," the man from the *American and Commercial Advertiser* expressed, "with its handsome carpet, ample room and easy chairs, is a luxury that the fraternity is not often blessed with." Appreciation was expressed as well for Prof. Almon Menter's orchestra which always gave a free concert nightly before the performance.

Rice's pair of horses, Excelsior and Stephen A. Douglas, received special commendation. It was suggested that their ideal forms might be studied as models by the artist who wished to chisel a horse out of white marble. But most astonishing was their marvelous intelligence. "Col. Rice indulges in none of those fantastic motions by which ordinary trainers put their horses through their role of tricks, but he quietly takes his stand, addresses the horse in the language that he would use to one of his assistants, if he wanted him to do the same thing, and the horse seems to comprehend the meaning of his words, and to act

---

63. New York *Clipper*, October 7, 1871, p. 214.

accordingly."[64]

The *Morning Sun* was every bit as appreciative. It was observed that the pavilion was "tastefully arranged inside, and exceedingly comfortable, being warmed and admirably lighted." Chandeliers and grand burners, that threw a flood of illumination on the ring, heightened the effect of the spectacle.[65]

The furnaces used for heating the pavilion were put to the test on the 17th. A cooling trend made it necessary to warm the place to an average temperature of 65°, rendering the audience "as comfortable as though they were sitting in their own houses."

A family matinee was given on Saturday, November 18th, and again on the following Wednesday. The admissions to all parts of the pavilion were reduced to 50¢ for adults and 25¢ for children. Additional attractions were brought in during this run. On the evening of the 18th, the English clown, James Cooke, first appeared. A few days later Prof. Davis was featured with his educated canines, which were trained to read from a book, perform acrobatic feats, walk a slack-rope, dance, form pyramids, etc. The run was extended to Thanksgiving Day, November 30th. At that time three performances were given, the one at 10:00 a.m. to accommodate the 18 teachers and pupils of the public schools for which prices were lowered to 25¢ in all parts of the house.

November 30th marked the end for the unique

---

64. Baltimore *American and Commercial Advertiser*, November 16, 1871, p. 4.

65. Baltimore *Morning Sun*, November 14, 1871, p. 2.

structure that had been developed for use at the Paris Exposition of 1867. The Pavilion, along with its cushy seats and opulent features, was placed in storage at James M. Eppley and Messrs. Morgan & Sons on North Howard Street.

The commentary from local papers had been consistent throughout the tour. As one newspaper man put it, "Gas, sofas, easy chairs, carpeted floors, and a good performance, all aid in making the visitor well pleased." The appearance and comfort within the pavilion was found to be far superior to anything seen at a circus before, with all seats numbered and sold by "coupon tickets," except for the family circle. An item in the Albany *Argus* bluntly affirmed that "pine boards as a substitute for chairs have had their natural effect, until the circus in this country has become anything but a favorable resort."[66] But equipped with cane-bottomed seats and settees and with parquet and boxes to separate them from the rowdy *hoi polloi*, people of respectability seldom seen at a show of this nature attended the Paris Pavilion. And, lastly, the twelve-act program offered by Rice was unique, pleasing, and beautifully presented. It was universally admired by the press and, if we can believe their accounts, well attended by a satisfied public.

Still, Rice's Grand Paris Pavilion Circus was a failure despite the apparent good business at the box office and its artistic success as expressed by the local newspapers. It is said that the proprietors lost some $60,000

---

66. Albany *Argus*, August 21, 1871, p. 4.

during the season. Quite simply, the Paris Pavilion was just too expensive to troupe. We know that it was used in places where the stands were for more than a single day, such as Detroit, Buffalo, Rochester, Syracuse, Troy, Albany, Brooklyn, and New York City.

It has been written that, closely-packed, the outfit filled ten of the largest-sized freight cars and that an extra heavy force of experienced working men was required to make the move.[67] We know that before the show opened in Baltimore several weeks were spent in improving the ground on Linden Avenue where the pavilion was to be erected.[68] We also know that it took a number of days to erect on site, perhaps a week at the very least. In Buffalo an item in the *Daily Courier*, four days in advance of the opening, read as follows: "Those who have passed up Main within a few days as far as the vacant lot on the corner of Virginia Street must have noticed the putting together of a curious looking structure and many have doubt-

---

67. St. Louis *Missouri Democrat*, April 9, 1871, p. 4.

68. Cincinnati *Enquirer*, August 28, 1874, p. 2. Rice's 1871 route (some dates are missing)—April: St. Louis, Missouri, 17th-29th. May: Kankakee, Illinois, 12th; Chicago, 15th-27th; Niles, Michigan 30th; Kalamazoo, 31st. June: Battle Creek, 1st; Ann Arbor, 5th; Detroit, 7th-10th; Toledo, Ohio, 14th-15th; Norwalk, 17th; Akron, 22nd; Warren, 23rd; Youngstown, 24th; Meadville, Pennsylvania, 26th; Franklin, 27th; Oil City, 28th. July: Titusville, 1st; Buffalo, New York, 6th-8th; Tonawanda, 10th; Niagara Falls, 11th; Lockport, 12th; Rochester, 17th-20th; Canandaigua, 21st; Clifton Springs, 22nd; Geneva, 24th; Auburn, 25th; Syracuse, 26th-28th; Oneida, 29th; Utica 31st. August: Herkimer, 1st; Little Falls, 2nd; Fort Plain, 3rd; Amsterdam, 4th; Schenectady, 5th; Troy, 7th-9th; Hoosick Falls, 10th; Saratoga Springs, 11th-12th; Albany, 21st-24th. September: Brooklyn, 4th-15th; Newark, New Jersey, 17th-18th; New York City, 25th-30th. October: New York City (continued), 2nd-7th. November: Baltimore, 13th-25th.

less been anxious to know what it all meant. Now that the canopy is over it it will readily occur to everybody that it is Dan Rice's grand Paris Pavilion in which he is to give a series of entertainments commencing on the afternoon of the 5th."[69]

How then could Rice tour this ponderous show as he did, making many one-day stands along the route? An auxiliary tent was carried for the one-day stands, while a large crew of workmen went ahead to prepare the ground and erect the Pavilion in the larger cities. The elaborate amphitheatre is not mentioned in either the advertising or the newspaper readers for these single day dates. According to the Utica *Daily Observer*, many of the citizens who turned out for the circus were disappointed in not seeing the Paris Pavilion "with its reserved seats and private boxes, and were almost discouraged from entering when they thought of the hard timber the common seats of a circus are made of."[70] The paper also revealed that Rice made no street parade. "His exhibition under the canvass requires no advertising of this character. It is worth the price of admission to see and hear Dan, the great American clown."[71] It is possible that the Apollonicon used for the street bally was left on its railroad car for these towns.

Were there open dates that were costly to Rice? If so, why one-day stands were not always used while the Pavilion was being erected in a major city is a mystery.

69. Buffalo *Daily Courier*, July 1, 1871, p. 2.

70, Utica *Daily Observer*, August 1, 1871, p. 3.

71. *Ibid.*, July 31, 1871, p. 3.

But for whatever reason there were gaps in the itinerary. As previously stated, after the season's opening in St. Louis, there were two weeks within which only one date was reported before the Chicago stand. Another example was the respite between Saratoga Springs and Albany. The former was played on the 11th and 12th of August; the Albany appearance on the 21st. But as indicated by an item in the *Argus* of that date, "Dan Rice and company arrived from Saratoga last evening."[72] That would be on the 20th, a full week later.

After closing in Baltimore, the Dan Rice circus set out under the optional canvas outfit for an extensive tour of the South, still under the title of Rice's Paris Pavilion Circus, but stripped of its real identity. The canvas pavilion was pitched in Norfolk, Virginia, on Gray Street, almost in the center of the city, for performances on December 4th, 5th, and 6th. Along with Rice, the advertising still listed Lizzie Marcellus, Lorenzo Mayo, the Nelson family, William H. Morgan, Fred O'Brien, William G. Miles, and Dick Clark, all members of the troupe when it left St. Louis a half-year since. The Baltimore arrivals, James Cooke and Prof. Davis and his seven performing dogs, remained with the tour. New to the roster were Billy Burko, described as a pantomime clown and "funniest of all fools;" W. W. Nichols, somersault rider; and Frank Gardner, rider, leaper, and gymnast. Admission prices were fixed at $1 for adults and 50¢ for children, double what was usual in the North. Except for Mentor's band, which

---

72. Albany *Argus*, August 21, 1871, p. 4.

gave a concert prior to the performances, there was no outside display. The interior was lighted by gas. The cold weather necessitated the use of furnaces within the canvas which, according to the Mobile *Daily Register*, made the place "as comfortable as any theatre." We assume that both the gas lighting fixtures and the heating units were the ones that had been used in Baltimore.

The show set up in Charleston, South Carolina, for a week beginning December 25th, Rice's first visit to the city since 1850. The clown's generosity was heralded by the *Daily Courier* after his agent dealt out passes to the "typos" of that newspaper. "The boys were so glad that joy beamed from their countenances," a writer exaggerated, "as they put their 'precious memorials' of Dan's philanthropy in their pocket, and went to their cases muttering blessings on the head of the Prince of the 'Paris Pavilion'."[73] An item indicated that the tent was attended by an audience largely composed of ladies, "whose delicate ears were saluted with nothing that could possibly put a blush on their fair cheeks."[74] Orphan children of the city, irrespective of "race, color, or previous condition," were guests at the Saturday matinee.

The tour continued for another month. The routing took the show into North and South Carolina, Georgia, Mississippi, and Alabama, then ended at Mobile for an advertised four days beginning January 22nd. No

---

73. Charleston *Daily Courier*, December 25, 1871, p. 1.

74. *Ibid.*, December 28, 1871, p. 1.

performances were given on the 25th, however, because of inclement weather. Two more days, the 26th and 27th, were added to the stand, for which the Fiji Cannibals were a new attraction; but, unfortunately, a cold, drizzling rain, which left the streets muddy to the extreme, spoiled these closing nights. On January 28th the Rice outfit was set up in New Orleans at Trivoli Square, the first of various locations in that city that would be visited until closing on February 23rd. And so, farewell!

The circus equipment that was stored in Baltimore remained there until 1873, when it was transferred to another warehouse until it was put up for auction to cover the storage charges on Monday, August 24, 1874. On this day, a crowd of about 500 people attended, primarily made up of the curious who often gather at similar functions, and the bargain hunters, or, to be more explicit, junk dealers.

Three years in storage had not improved the value of this circus property. Several tents and a large number of seats were in shabby condition—the chairs being moldy and the canvas so rotten that it was unsuitable for anything but paper mill stock. On the other hand, much of the carpeting, most of which had been stored in boxes, was in good condition.

The bidding was at no time heavy and the returns were what one might expect. About 1,000 of the cane-bottomed chairs in fairly good condition sold for 35¢ each, five hundred of the settees for 37½¢ each; tent poles, gas fixtures, and old carpeting, put up together, $150; about 3,000 pounds of old canvas, comprising several small tents, 10½¢ per pound; 300 pounds of Brussels carpeting which had been used in the ring, $34 for the lot; a complete small tent, $9; 500 yards of royal velvet carpet used for the parquet and the private boxes brought $1.65 a yard; and several other odds and ends probably totaled $100. The final result of the sale could not have added up to more than $2,500, far short of the original cost of the items, which was estimated between $10,000 and $13,000.[75] So much for Rice's noble experiment, dismembered and forgotten, as its artifacts faded into anonymity.

---

75. Rochester *Evening Express*, August 28, 1874, p. 1. The same account was carried in the Cincinnati *Enquirer*, August 28, 1874, p. 2.

# STRANGE BEDFELLOWS
## THE POGEY O'BRIEN INTERVAL, 1874-1875

The 1874 circus under P. T. Barnum's name went out under new management because the regular Barnum team was occupied with another venture. Although we have no intention of fully particularizing this change of direction—our main interest here being with the circus—a brief description might prove beneficial.

The Barnum organization took a bold turn this year by launching P. T. Barnum's New Roman Hippodrome, which was not a circus. There were no center rings as we know them. There were no clowns and but a few of the variety performances recognizable as circus acts. Instead, there was a large hippodrome track for racing horses, camels, elephants, and most anything else with legs. And with the track and the infield created by its oval, there was space for huge spectacle displays.

In his autobiography, Barnum referred to a "long-cherished plan of exhibiting a Roman Hippodrome, Zoological Institute, Aquaria, and Museum of unsurpassing extent and magnificence." His propensity for topping his previous achievements, strengthened by the financial success of the 1873 circus tenting season, supported the acceptance of such a scheme.

Plans for his last "crowning effort" were set in motion in the fall of 1873. Barnum left for Europe in September and while there visited all the zoological gardens, circuses, and public exhibitions wherever he went, acquiring various novelties and valuable ideas. He then moved on to England where on January $2^{nd}$ he contracted with John and George Sanger to purchase duplicates of the entire wardrobe and paraphernalia connected with the "Congress of Monarchs," an impressive spectacle that had been exhibited at Agricultural Hall, London, some years earlier.

Meanwhile, his assistants, Coup and Hurd, leased the New York and Harlem Railroad Company property in New York City at Fourth Avenue and $26^{th}$ Street that had been left vacant in 1871 by the opening of Grand Central Station at $42^{nd}$ Street, and set about constructing a suitable venue. When the place opened to the public on April 27, 1874, the list of officialdom included P. T. Barnum, proprietor; W. C. Coup, general manager; S. H. Hurd, superintendent and treasurer; and Dan Castello, director of amusements.

The venture got off to a successful start. Newspaper advertisements claimed an average daily attendance of 20,000, with thousands unable to gain admission for the evening performance.[76] This may have been an overstatement; but the place, which on completion seated somewhere between 10,000 and 12,000 specta-

---

76. Advertisement, New York *Times*, May 16, 1874.

tors, was reported to have been filled almost nightly until the season closed on August 1st.

The Connecticut Legislature issued a charter for the P. T. Barnum Universal Exposition Company, with a capital of a million dollars, on July 24, 1874. Barnum was recorded as president; W. C. Coup, as manager. Under the aegis of this enterprise, the immense Roman Hippodrome, with its aggregate of some four- to five-hundred men, women, and children, four-hundred horses, and an assortment of camels, elephants and other quadrupeds, went on tour to introduce its unparalleled marvels to audiences outside of New York City, namely Boston, Philadelphia, Baltimore, Pittsburgh, and Cincinnati.

An advance crew of carpenters and other specialists preceded the show by several days in order to level the ground, prepare the hippodrome track and construct a tiered amphitheatre around it. The practice of erecting a wooden structure for seating at each stand in advance of arrival had been instigated by Barnum's circus manager to some degree the previous year.

Following the Hippodrome's final performance on October 24th, the weather being too cold to continue on to St. Louis and Chicago, the outfit was shipped back to New York City. All in all, the season had offered the most luxurious show of pageantry ever attempted on this continent. The various races contributed to a continuous excitement throughout the entirety of the matinee and evening programs. The claim of performing to 20,000 people a day was not disturbingly far from the truth. Barnum's "crowning effort," at least for this year, had been a crowning success.

Embarking on the Hippodrome project meant leaving idle a successful circus with accompanying equipment too new and too valuable to sacrifice at auction prices. The solution was to lease the title and equipment to another showman, along with the Barnum curiosities and many of the employees. The new manager of P. T. Barnum's Great Traveling Museum, Menagerie and World's Fair for the seasons of 1874 and 1875 was John V. "Pogey" O'Brien.

The choice of O'Brien to carry on the three-year-old Barnum circus name has raised more than a few eyebrows over the years. Skeptics have asked why a man of Barnum's stature would select a partner of such questionable integrity, a man whose legacy is the image of a scoundrel, who throughout a lengthy career in management developed a notoriety for dishonesty, coarseness, and a tolerance for grifters, qualities consistently purported by circus people and circus historians. And we have accepted them as representing the true nature of Pogey O'Brien. For example, C. G. Sturtevant wrote: "…he took mean advantage of his people, in small ways to mulct them of money they had due. He was also notorious in beating everyone he possibly could with whom he came in contact. His shows were a paradise for grifters, not in the ordinary sense of the word, for at the time many others carried grift with some discrimination, but on the O'Brien shows it was wide open. Gamblers, thieves and all manner of thugs were carried, and had protection both by fixers and a celebrated gang of canvasmen known as the 'Irish Brigade,' which were recruited with regard for their ability and love for a fight. This gang of iron-fisted bruisers never lost a decision in the numerous clems the show got into with an outraged public."[77]

D. W. Watt, treasurer for the Forepaugh circus in the 1880s, accused O'Brien of knowing "little about the Ten Commandments." Chindahl, in his book, *The History of the Circus in America,* stated: "If John V. Pogey O'Brien deserves mention in a history of the American circus, it is because he was a notable example of the dishonesty toward both employees and the public which characterized many shows. Gamblers and thieves became integral parts of his activities."[78]

Unfortunately, all of the above, although consistent in their charges, list no sources.

History has left us with little personal knowledge of this man O'Brien. We know he was born on January 29, 1836, the son of an Irish stonemason and resident of Frankford, Pennsylvania, a suburb of Philadelphia. Beyond that, only two accounts by contemporaries supply us with most of what else we know, both

---

77. Sturtevant, C. G., "Little Biographies of Famous American Circus Men," in *White Tops*, February, 1929, p. 4.

78. Chindahl, George L., *A History of the Circus in America*, p. 103. There are, occasionally, specific references to O'Brien malpractice. In 1878, for example, Linda Jeal and her husband, William O'Dale Stevens, were in O'Brien's Campbell's Circus, but after leaving in late August had to sue to get their horse and wardrobe properties returned (John Daniel Draper, "Linda Jeal and Her Equestrian Kin," in *Bandwagon*, May-June, 1987, p. 31).

written by former employees, one being submitted to the New York *Clipper* in 1872 by Birkit Clarke, who was O'Brien's treasurer the previous year.[79] Stuart Thayer speculates that some of what Clarke wrote was designed to ingratiate him with O'Brien as a means of future employment. I leave that to the reader to determine.

Clarke tells us that O'Brien's education was acquired more from physical combat with his schoolmates than from an open textbook. From such lack of devotion to learning, father O'Brien concluded that his son was more fit for labor than scholarship; so he put him to work mixing plaster. The job lasted until one day a larger boy threw an apple core at him, which ignited a bit of serious fisticuffs with John coming off the winner, only to receive a disheartening thrashing from his father. This may have been the catalyst that caused his running away from home.[80]

The mature O'Brien, Clarke recalls, was a man free with everybody—"a king or a canvasman would be all the same to him." He was always in good humor and his fund of anecdotes was endless. He was an enthusiastic "kidder," then, after committing some such trickery, would explode with laughter.[81]

The other contemporary from whom we learn about O'Brien is George Conklin, who left us with the best

---

79. Clarke, Birkit, "Among the Showmen," in New York *Clipper*, January 13, 1872, p. 324.

80. *Ibid.*

81. *Ibid.*

picture of him in his book *The Ways of the Circus*.[82] Conklin joined on with O'Brien in 1867 and was with him for several years, eventually becoming the show's animal man. He obviously knew Pogey better than most of his contemporaries. In *The Ways of the Circus* he described the man as "rough and illiterate, yet with a large stock of native shrewdness." He remembered him as being fat and good-natured, but a rough-and-tough character, unable to read or write, but, as he termed it, "hell on figures." He suffered from asthma which revealed itself in his wheezing voice and peculiar laugh and required his sleeping in a chair instead of a bed. He touched neither tobacco nor hard liquor. He found pleasure in attracting attention through his opulent attire, usually appearing in a frock coat, pants made of blue broadcloth, and a velvet vest. For hiring performers he changed to a double-breasted vest with two rows of buttons inlaid with diamonds, from which hung a large watch chain with each gold link set in precious stones as well.[83] Press agent Charles H. Day recalled that whenever O'Brien stayed in New York City, he slept on a sofa in the lobby of the St. Charles Hotel to save a dollar.[84] This miserly quality was both an attribute and a weakness.

At barely seventeen O'Brien became a stage driver in Philadelphia which lasted for a half-dozen years, during which time, through a life of frugality, he bought

---

82. Conklin, George, *The Ways of the Circus*, p. 22-28.

83. *Ibid.*

84. Day, Charles H., "Happy Days at the St. Charles," in *Billboard*, November 5, 1904.

horses on the side. He then moved to Washington, D.C., where he drove a stage between that city and Alexandria, Virginia, and ultimately became owner or part-owner in the line. He entered the circus business in 1861 by renting horses to Gardner & Hemmings and going along as boss hostler. The next year he owned one third interest in the show and retained it until he sold it to James E. Cooper a few weeks into the 1863 season. He then organized his own show that year, Bryan's (sometimes referred to as Brian's) National Circus with Mrs. Dan Rice, for touring in Pennsylvania and New York state. Clarke states that "from all I have heard regarding the concern, it must have been a very 'light-waisted' affair."[85] But, let it be noted, the show made money.

In 1864 O'Brien took out the Tom King Excelsior Circus with the leaper Tom King as the star. This was a partnership between O'Brien and Adam Forepaugh's man on the lot. It came about because Forepaugh had earlier supplied show horses, but when the payment came due he was forced to accept a share of the circus as settlement. After a route through Pennsylvania, Ohio, and Michigan, King left the show in Port Huron on August 20th because of a disagreement. On September 3rd a card appeared in the advertising columns of the *Clipper*: "Having withdrawn from the associate management of O'Brien & King's Excelsior Circus, I take this method of requesting Mr. O'Brien to remove my name from the top of the bills…. I will give

---

85. Clarke, *op. cit.*, p. 324.

him twenty days from this date to do this. There are several honorable men in the Company, but I am sorry I ever associated myself with an omnibus driver—Tom King."[86]

This appears to be the first negative imprint on O'Brien's reputation as a manager.

The O'Brien-Forepaugh partnership continued in 1865, when in April of that year the two men purchased the Jerry Mabie menagerie, consisting of twelve cages, two elephants and other animals. It was delivered at Twelfth and State Streets, Chicago, on the very day of the assassination of President Lincoln. This became the Dan Rice Menagerie.

The managers eventually found they could not get along, so the partnership was dissolved after the 1865 season. According to Conklin, they divided the property by each man alternately selecting a wagon or an animal or some piece of equipment, a process that continued throughout the entire circus inventory.[87] For the 1866 season O'Brien leased his animals to Yankee Robinson under George W. Sears' supervision, but there is no evidence that he took a circus on the road. Forepaugh went out again under the Dan Rice title.

With the split, O'Brien increased his circus activity by acquiring more circus property. In 1867 he organized Whithy & Co., which included a menagerie, while again Yankee Robinson leased the so-called Mabie animals. In 1868 he owned both Bryan's Circus

---

86. New York *Clipper*, September 3, 1864, p. 167.

87. Conklin, *op. cit.*, p. 25.

and Menagerie and DeMott & Ward's. In 1869 he operated Bryan's again, as well as Campbell's Circus and Menagerie, the latter managed by Hyatt Frost. These two shows were out again under the management of James DeMott. His fifty cage menagerie that year was the largest in the country. Throughout these years he amassed so much property that in 1871 he put four outfits on the road, each with a menagerie—John O'Brien's Sheldenberger's, Hardenberger & Co.'s, and J. E. Warner & Co.'s. In 1872 he had three shows, O'Brien's, J. E. Warner & Co.'s, and Kleckner & Co's.

O'Brien had a circus under his own name in 1873, which, perhaps in imitation of Barnum's Great Traveling World's Fair, was called John O'Brien's World's Fair on Wheels. The show exhibited under six round tops of canvas, five of which were described as "the worse for wear." The performing tent, however, was new. The menagerie was still the feature attraction, being made up of thirty-five cages. He also had interest in the Rice, Ryan & Spalding Circus that year. By now he was looked upon as a wealthy man and one of the most successful circus proprietors in the United States.

When he became associated with Barnum he was young and experienced in the business, having been in management for ten years, longer than either Coup or Castello before they teamed with Barnum in 1871. In Clarke's 1872 article he was described as having a remarkable knowledge of show business. He possessed an elegant mansion in Frankford, Pennsylvania. Two blocks away his animal buildings covered an acre of ground and his nearby farm contained 500 head of stock. He was a perfect picture of an energetic and successful entrepreneur. And, with his large collection of animals, like Barnum, he was a man more interested in exhibition than performance. So, O'Brien, in 1874, at age thirty-eight, would have been considered nothing less than an experienced and successful showman, capable of succeeding the team of Coup, Castello, and Hurd.

But if his reputation for dishonesty has merit, and one has to believe it does, what justified Barnum's association with him? Barnum, who was so sensitive about establishing his own image as a paragon of virtue and the circus under his name as a great moral institution, would never have accepted a partnership with someone of what we now consider an unseemly reputation. I can only conclude that it had not become a factor by 1874.

I refer to Clarke again. "Wherever he is known his word is equivalent to his note," Clarke attested in 1872, and "in excellent health, with ample wealth, and with an interesting family about him, he has all that can make a man happy in this world."[88] As late as 1880, George H. Batcheller and John B. Doris, who had been associated with O'Brien enterprises for eleven seasons, entered a card of appreciation in the New York *Clipper* which read in part: "In all transactions of whatever nature, we have always found you to be just and honor-

---

88. Clarke, *op. cit.*, p. 324.

able, while large experience and sound judgment have been of incalculable benefit to us."[89]

O'Brien's negative image, a result of cumulative improprieties, must have been formed after Barnum's selection of him as a partner.

Little has been made of the two years of O'Brien's tenure under the Barnum title. Arthur Saxon, the preeminent Barnum biographer, makes slight mention of it, and Barnum, who was far more attentive to the fortunes of the Great Roman Hippodrome, was equally remiss in his autobiography. We know that, unlike the 1873 Barnum circus, this show moved on wagons but maintained the familiar elements of the previous circuses under the Barnum name. The two-ring format, originated by Coup in 1872, remained. The main tent seated some 5,000 spectators. The Barnum autobiography was still on sale and still reduced to $1.50. The customary Barnum logo appeared on most of the advertising and Barnum's presence was felt even in his absence: "The happy face of Phineas Taylor Barnum has smiled so benignly upon *Observer* patrons during the past fortnight," the Utica *Daily Observer* read, "that all have anxiously awaited the advent of his traveling world."[90] And the bills spelled out the typical Barnum line: "The Great Object Teacher of the Masses," "With Over 1,000 Assistants, Now Presenting 100,000 Life Lessons." The level of ring artistry was on a par with most of the major circuses. The museum and menagerie

---

89. New York *Clipper*, November 13, 1880, p. 272.

90. Utica *Daily Observer*, September 17, 1874, p. 3.

were still featured over the ring performance. Many of the curiosities of the previous years were on exhibit—Admiral Dot, the Fiji Cannibals, a Circassian Lady, the talking machine, etc. James L. "Doctor" Thayer, the clown and ex-circus proprietor, represented Barnum's interest with the show.

The ring performances were under the equestrian management of James Cooke, the well-known English jester. The leading equestrians were James Melville and sons and Lucille Watson. They were supported by Arthur Nelson and his family of acrobats, the clowning and stilt-walking Jerry Hopper, and the educated goat, Alexis. In addition, Herr Lippard showed his mastery over some number of "brute actors"—a collection of Phi Beta Kappa ponies, dogs and monkeys. Dan Castello's trained horse, Senator, and his comic mules, Pete and Barney, having no place with the Hippodrome, were part of O'Brien's lease, as were the museum wagons and many of the cages and their contents.

The show confined its 1874 tour to the Northeast. After opening in Frankford, there were a number of stands in New Jersey and, for a few weeks in mid-July, in Canada; but most of the season was devoted to Pennsylvania and New York states. One might add that for both the 1874 and 1875 seasons O'Brien did not exhibit in New York City or its environs as had the previous circuses under Barnum's name. Rather, he stayed shy of the major cities as well as the areas in which the Roman Hippodrome was routed.

The 1875 season opened at Washington, D.C., for

a week beginning April 12th, which turned out to be the only major stand. The arenic program featured the carrying act of Martinho Lowande and his young son, Tony; Madame Elisa Dockrill, the beautiful equestrienne; the gymnastic Leslie Brothers; and the clown, William H. Porter. Most of the season was spent visiting the medium and smaller size cities in Pennsylvania and Ohio, with a few dates in New Jersey and Kentucky. Norristown, Pennsylvania, closed the tour on October 21st before the show went into winter quarters at Newark, New Jersey.

The season over, the Barnum/O'Brien relationship was terminated and the animals and equipment from both units were put up for auction. Unfortunately for O'Brien the Panic of 1873 lasted until 1878, and not only was business bad, he lost $9,400 in the collapse of the Jay Cooke bank. The lease ended on a sour note and Barnum was forced to sue for a $14,000 shortfall. To make matters worse, Adam Forepaugh took Barnum to court in 1879 for the value of the property sold as belonging to O'Brien—horses, wagons, cages, etc.—claiming the property was really his.

The Barnum name did not draw as well as in previous years. A scribe for the Cleveland *Herald* explained it by stating O'Brien "tried to make the public believe that he was a 'genuine Barnum,' but it was like the equine quadruped which put on the lion's skin—the ears were too long."[91]

The second year of P. T. Barnum's Great Roman

---

91. Clipping, Cleveland *Herald*, December 22, 1875, n.p.n.

Hippodrome also ended in failure. The attempt to operate the show similar to a one night stand circus was a mistake; the large and cumbersome outfit was just too expensive. With this the Coup and Barnum partnership came to an end. It has been suggested that Coup's departure was provoked by some animosity between the two. Coup never made a public statement to confirm this; and if there was resentment it was probably of minor concern. Still, there were contemporary rumors. An item in an 1875 Cleveland *Herald* suggested that Coup had seen impending trouble two years earlier and "tried several times to slip out of the concern."[92] Such inferences may have caused Barnum to make the following qualification in his Advance Courier of 1876: "In reply to many inquiries regarding my friend and late manager, Mr. W. C. Coup, I wish to say, that having labored hard and 'made his pile,' he preferred to retire, at least for a season. Meanwhile our friendship is uninterrupted. Mr. Coup is an efficient manager and a scrupulously honest and upright gentleman."[93]

The Barnum/O'Brien partnership experienced problems and a general lack of success in management from the outset. For example, a sojourn into Canada during mid-summer of 1874 was a financial disaster. In retrospect, the Great Traveling World's Fair was merely the usual O'Brien offering, barely held aloft by Barnum's name and famous logo. And Barnum, who during his

---

92. *Ibid.*

93. 1876 Barnum Advance Courier, p. 4.

first three years in circus management was so instrumental in exciting immense public interest, was more involved in promoting his Roman Hippodrome than his circus. This was reflected by the local press, which devoted great splashes of ink extolling the wonders of the former and gave only superficial attention to the latter.

Conklin has written that O'Brien owed salary to "Doc" Thayer at season's end, but when Thayer asked for his money, he responded with, "Get it out of Barnum." This refusal to pay up would prove costly. While the show was in Canada in 1874 O'Brien had replaced his run-down horses with fresh stock. On his return to the United States he did not report the exchange to the custom officers, but passed through duty-free. An angry Thayer threatened to report him unless he made good on the unpaid salary.

"I don't care. Tell all yer want ter. I ain't scared," was O'Brien's reply.

So Thayer did just that. The result was a lawsuit by the government against O'Brien over the unpaid duties which dragged out for two or three years, with O'Brien eventually having to make good on the claim as well as hefty court fees.[94]

We can only surmise that O'Brien's years of good fortune had peaked by 1874. In all probability, his financial setbacks were serious enough to encourage desperate tactics for acquiring the "almighty dollar" by every means available to him. And, by all accounts,

---

94. Conklin, *op. cit.*, p. 31.

he did. The sad portrait of Pogey O'Brien encompasses a fun-loving Irishman who raised himself to wealth from nothing through a natural shrewdness and toughness in business dealings, only to revert to his primitive origins, ruthlessly fighting over every apple core, and willing to profit from the vulnerability of others, thereby leaving a legacy of dishonor.

# TWO RINGS AND A HIPPODROME TRACK

From the very beginnings of the American circus there was what could be called a "one-ring mentality" with both circus people and with the general public. The earliest indoor circus venues, in Europe and in America, were circular, erected to encompass a single ring. Because the ring was the sole focus for audiences and because construction space was a premium concern, the seating area abutted the ring curbing. This arrangement created an intimacy between audience and performer and allowed for equitable viewing from every seat in the amphitheatre.

When circuses adapted the canvas pavilion for moving about the country, the round tops imitated the configuration of the permanent buildings. The single ring within a small circular enclosure, then, was thoroughly ingrained as the standard form for circus performance, and represented this "one-ring mentality" that was prevalent up to and throughout the 1870s.

Many of us have been under assumption that P. T. Barnum's Great Traveling World's Fair originated the use of a second ring for circus performances in 1872.

In part, the confusion was caused by the Barnum advertising for that year that frequently included the line: "The first and only show in the world that uses a double circus ring, and requires a double circus troupe of performers." Such a reference can be found in newspapers from Clinton, Iowa, to Baltimore, Maryland. In the Toledo *Blade*, for example, it was stated that "there are seen at one time in the great double ring, in the Grand Entrée Pageant, one hundred performers," etc.[95] The Lodi, Wisconsin *Journal* included a reference to "a double set of performers, a double circus ring." But notice that the term "double ring" is used, rather than "two rings." The former could be interpreted to mean one inside the other, the latter to mean rings side by side. Be that as it may, it is understandable why the notion of a two-ring performance was erroneously accepted.[96]

I will show that there were not two rings with simultaneous performances with the Barnum show, or any other circus, in 1872; but that it was 1873 when the two-ring circus was first used.

For the Barnum's 1872 opener at the Empire Rink in New York City, there was but one performing ring. In reporting on it, the New York *Clipper* noted that the living curiosities were "exhibited in the ring at the commencement of the circus performances," with no

---

95. Toledo *Blade*, June 29, 1872, n.p.n.

96. The idea was perpetuated by C. Fred Crosby in his article, "The Early Days of Barnum's 'Greatest on Earth'," in *Billboard*, January 21, 1922, p. 49.

mention of a second ring.[97] In referring to the circus in Cleveland, the *Plain Dealer* contained the line, "Dan Castello's famous circus (which was the performing wing of the Barnum show), under the care and direction of that veteran himself, occupies the ring."[98] The *Ring*. One cannot find a reference to two rings in either the Barnum 1872 route book or Advance Courier. Nor is there a reference in the full page ad placed in the *Clipper* at the outset of the 1872 season, which contains Barnum's forty-seven challenges.[99] Out of those many boasts, you would think two rings would have been included if there were two.

Our conclusion, and one we will continue to support in this paper, is that the second ring inference relates to the increased space between the ring and the audience, created by the use of a larger canvas pavilion to accommodate an extended seating area. This space, which formed a ring around the ring, was for circuses the origin of what we now refer to as the hippodrome track. Therefore, the true explanation for the advertisements of two rings in 1872 is that there was a new performing area around the single ring that could be used for greater spectacle.

There are contemporary illustrations to support this view. A small engraving in the 1872 Barnum Advance Courier shows the Grand Entrée, entitled "The Halt in the Desert," being paraded within the single ring. Although this supports our one-ring theory, it is of no

---

97. New York *Clipper*, April 13, 1872, p. 14.

98. Cleveland *Plain Dealer*, April 13, 1872, p. 14.

99. New York *Clipper*, April 19, 1872, p. 24.

help in confirming the use of an outer ring for spectacle. Our explanation is that the same Grand Entrée was used in 1871 and that the engraving was made for the 1871 season and carried over into the 1872.

From the Morris H. Porter photograph of the exterior of the tent, taken in Kalamazoo, Michigan, on October 24, 1872, we know that there were two center-poles and a canvas middle piece of some fifty or more feet, ideal for a single ring.

But even more convincing is a stereoview of the tent's interior, entered into the Library of Congress in 1873 by A. W. Anderson, which graphically reveals a single ring surrounded by usable space between it and the tiers of seating.[100] This has to be the 1872 tent because only a single center-pole was used in 1871 and, as we will show later, there were decidedly two rings and three center-poles in 1873.

The gist of the 1872 advertisements was repeated in 1873 when three rings were prominently proclaimed. Newspapers referred to three circus troupes and three separate and distinct rings, seen by the whole audience simultaneously. For example, an article in the Cleveland *Plain Dealer* stated there would be "three rings and at times there [would] be performances in all three at once."[101] The Buffalo *Daily Courier* confirmed this with: "Under the vast Hippodrome Pavilion are three rings, one of which is used entirely for the Grand Oriental Pageant, and the others for the performances

---

100. Original copies in the Albert Conover collection, Circus World Museum.

101. Cleveland *Plain Dealer*, July 14, 1873, p. 3.

that follow. In the two rings two acts go on simultaneously, but the salient and brilliant features of the act in one ring are so admirably timed with reference to those in the other that confusion is entirely avoided."[102] And the Jackson, Michigan *Daily Citizen* reiterated: "in this tent there are three separate and distinct circus rings, with three separate and distinct sets of performers and performances, all in progress at the same time."[103] The New York *Clipper*, reporting on the Boston stand, stated that "the novelty of seeing three rings in action at once is alone worth the price of admission."[104] Note the word "novelty."

The Advance Courier for 1873 stated: "Two of these arenas or circus rings will be in operation by two different sets of performances, at the same time… while the third vast ring, larger than either of the others, will be used exclusively for the Grand Entrée Pageant, Tournament, etc., and other spectacular demonstrations." The third ring, then, was what we now call the hippodrome track. From this, it is safe to assume that the second 1872 ring was not one of two rings where simultaneous performances were given; but rather, it was an outer ring in which, perhaps for the first time in America, the Grand Entrée expanded from the confinement of the performing ring to the origin of the hippodrome track.

At other times the 1873 ads mentioned only "grand double hippodrome performances in separate and

---

102. Buffalo *Daily Courier*, July 2, 1873, p. 3.
103. Jackson *Daily Citizen*, May 10, 1873, p. 4.
104. New York *Clipper*, May 24, 1873, p. 63.

distinct rings in full view of the audience."[105] The *Clipper* Supplement, in its annual preseason circus listings, revealed that: "A squad of twenty men under Charles McDean (*sic*) will go one day in advance to prepare the grounds and make the double rings used by this company."[106] The New York *Times*, in commenting on the first stand of the season at the American Institute (the Rink), observed that "two large rings are formed, and the audience occupies raised seats around them.... Similar performances occur simultaneously in each ring, so that the whole audience can see one or both, as it chooses."[107] From the Battle Creek, Michigan *Daily Journal*: "The performance comes off in two large rings."[108] An advertisement in the New York *Daily Graphic* included, "Two separate and distinct circus arenas in simultaneous performances."[109] The Pittsburgh *Post* commented about the center of the tent being "occupied by two large rings."[110] The *Clipper*, also reporting on the Pittsburgh date, revealed that "two rings and simultaneous performances in the circus were a new feature."[111] Again, I call your attention to the words "new feature," and be aware that the circus played Pittsburgh in 1872 as well. Concerning a four-day stand in Cincinnati, the *Clipper* reinforces

---

105. Providence *Daily Journal*, May 6, 1873, p. 3.

106. New York *Clipper* Supplement, April 19, 1873, p. 1.

107. New York *Times*, April 4, 1873, n.p.n.

108. Battle Creek *Daily Journal*, July 18, 1873, p. 4.

109. New York *Daily Graphic*, October 17, 1873, p. 760.

110. Pittsburgh *Post*, July 9, 1873, p. 4.

111. New York *Clipper*, July 19, 1873, p. 127.

our thesis with: "The show has been considerably enlarged since its visit last year, particularly in the circus department, where two rings are filled with a constant succession of performances of an unusually varied description."[112]

Barnum's 1873 Advance Courier stresses the double ring configuration and includes an artist's sketch of it, which also shows a hippodrome track. An engraving in the New York *Daily Graphic* of October 28, 1873, depicts simultaneous performances in two rings and a hippodrome track.

It is irrefutably true that the Barnum show of 1873 was the first to make use of two rings placed side-by-side. That is a given.

There is another, perhaps more compelling, reason for the misunderstanding about the number of rings in 1872. It is based on a statement made by W. C. Coup in his book, *Sawdust and Spangles*. His entry is open to misinterpretation. It is commonly known that the book attributed to Coup's authorship is a composite of dictated notes by him, which was published after his death. We have no assurance that the various entries are in chronological order or how one section connects to another. His two-ring statement comes in the opening sentence of a new section, the section title being "The Spartan Habits of the Old-Timers." It reads: "Our experience with the vast crowds of the season before had given us the idea of building two rings and

---

112. New York *Clipper*, August 2, 1873, p. 143.

giving a double performance."[113] Which season before? Granted the previous section describes the switch to rail transportation in 1872, which could lead one to believe that the following section is a continuance of the same year and the "year before" to which Coup referred was 1871, which would make 1872 the year he moved to two rings. But it is possible that the two sections are not time-connected, are not referring to the same year. It is unfortunate that Coup did not assemble his writing into a book himself and expand on the jottings that he put down.

Dan Castello, one of the Barnum partners at the time has been of no help in placing the year. His only statement regarding the two rings was within an article in a Syracuse paper: "Barnum came to me and asked what we were going to do, as the canvas was getting so big that the people could not see. I told him that we would have to put in two rings."[114] When did Barnum come to him? I have no idea. We do know the tent was longer for the season of 1872 by at the very least a middle piece, thereby putting the end seats at a greater distance than those on the sides; and, in so doing, creating a problem for the end-seated audiences.

This seating problem was referred to by Coup directly following his statement on adding a second ring. "This, of course, doubled our company, but it kept the audience in their seats, since they were precisely as well off in one part of the canvas as another, whereas

---

113. Coup, W. C., *Sawdust and Spangles*, p. 63.

114. Syracuse *Standard*, 1899, n.p.n. [clipping].

in the old one-ring show we found it impossible to prevent the people who were farthest from the ring from standing up. They would rush to the front and thus interfere with many other people."[115] They rushed to the front, we believe, because the addition of a middle piece that year, 1872, as we have said, created a greater distance from the ring for audiences placed in the end seats. But the purpose of the added canvas was not to make use of a second ring; it was to seat more people by enlarging the perimeter. In doing so the crowd-management problem was created.

This was corroborated by press agent Louis E. Cooke, who worked for the Barnum and Bailey organization for several years and who was also well acquainted with Coup. Cooke confirmed that the introduction of two rings came after the enlargement of the pavilion and from the necessity "to keep the people seated at the extreme ends of the big canvas, as it was found that with only one ring crowds on the end seats would become restless, leave their seats and rush to the center, making it impossible for the balance of the audience to see the performance."[116]

The adding of the second ring, as Coup said, doubled the company. But in looking at the performing roster for 1872, the year previously assumed the show had gone to two rings, we find little difference in the company's size from 1871. On the other hand, Stuart Thayer has described the 1873 program as one of the largest

---

115. Coup, *op. cit.*, p. 63.

116. Cooke, Louis E., "Reminiscences of a Showman," in Newark *Evening Star*, August 19, 1915, n.p.n.

seen to that time, with sixteen changes, all but three involving both rings."[117] Richard A. Arnold published the route books for both the 1872 and 1873 seasons. But only for 1873 are the acts shown as they appeared in both ring one and ring two.

Strong evidence establishes 1873 as the year of the first touring two-ring American circus. P. T. Barnum's Great Traveling World's Fair, a wagon show managed by John V. "Pogey" O'Brien, continued the practice for 1874. With that, the Barnum people did not use more than one ring until 1881 when the newly consolidated Barnum, Bailey & Co.'s Great London Show placed three rings side by side for the very first time in circus history.

---

117. Thayer, Stuart and William S. Slout, *Grand Entrée*. San Bernardino, CA: Borgo Press, p. 53.

# THE ADVENTURES OF JAMES M. NIXON, FORGOTTEN IMPRESARIO

James M. Nixon (1820-1899) was a showman of the nineteenth-century mold, with a career that was comparable in length to many of the great proprietors of that period—John F. Robinson, S. P. Stickney, George F. Bailey, Adam Forepaugh, etc. Under the influence of the indomitable P. T. Barnum (and what showman was not at that time), he used innovative tactics, issued what was described as "flaming, regardless of expense advertisements," engaged much of the finest talent available, and spread his managerial interests into several niches of public amusement. Odell referred to him at various times as "elegant," a "power," and "a wielder of big interests."

Press agent Charles H. Day once wrote of him, "Jim Nixon could furnish reminiscences enough of his own career to fill a volume and a right interesting one it would be, too." Yet, when he died in 1899, his obituary in the New York *Clipper* was not only inaccurate but inexcusably remiss in truly representing his accomplishments.[118] The flaming torch of James M. Nixon had tapered to a dark and smokeless wick.

Nixon worked his way from a mere groom with Aaron Turner's circus around 1836 to performing with various troupes in the 1840s and 1850s as acrobat, ringmaster and equestrian director. Although references to his early career are sketchy, we are able to follow a trail of professional activity (thanks to the persistent research efforts of Stuart Thayer[119]) that will eventually lead us to the more fertile years of circus chronicling.

Thayer tells us that from a Turner stable groom Nixon graduated to other menial tasks with the show—lamp trimmer, ring builder, and ultimately performer. How long he was with this circus is not known, since Turner did not habitually list the names of his company in the advertising. After leaving Turner, his whereabouts are a mystery until John Glenroy's reference to him on Welch & Mann's roster in the spring of 1843.[120] At that time, managers Welch and Mann divided their forces into two units. Rufus Welch took one and set sail in May on the brig *Francis Amy* for Mediterranean ports; Col. Alvah Mann opened at New York's Bowery

118. *Clipper*, September 30, 1899, p. 638: "James M. Nixon, an old time circus manager, died Sept. 16 at the Putnam House, this city, aged seventy-nine years. Nearly a half a century ago he was among the best known of the circus managers, and claimed to be the first one to take an American circus abroad. He made a great deal of money but lost most of his fortune in endeavoring to fight P. T. Barnum. He retired about twenty years ago. He leaves two children."

119. We refer to notes submitted to the author, as well as the outstanding three-volume series, *Annals of the American Circus*.

120. John H. Glenroy, *Ins and Outs of Circus Life*, p. 44.

Amphitheatre with the other in June. It is with the latter that Nixon performed as a $6.75-a-week acrobat.

The circus left the Bowery quarters on July 6th and moved to Brooklyn's Military Gardens for a week's stand. Here a deal was made for L. B. Lent and William A. Delavan to assume the management and take the company to Boston for five weeks; at the end of which, the circus returned to the Bowery Amphitheatre, now under the proprietorship of John Tryon. At this point, Nixon replaced John Shay as ringmaster.

Uncle John Tryon (1800-1876) was a native New Yorker who began professional life as a reporter for the *Herald*. Having at one point conducted a job-printing office, he is credited with composing the first illustrated show bill in this country, a single sheet with figures printed in black ink. He became a leading writer of copy for bills and other advertising; and, as a circus manager, his career extended over more than twenty-five years. He was a man of superior ability, an intelligent and scholarly individual, highly thought of by his colleagues and the general public.

We know that Tryon's managerial name was connected with the Bowery Amphitheatre from 1843 through 1848. We also know that Nixon was equestrian director for him in the winter of 1845. It may be that he was with Tryon in 1844 as well. Then, some time in the winter of 1845, Dr. G. R. Spalding put a show into the Bowery and Nixon remained as equestrian director.

Shortly before this, however, Nixon married his first

wife, Caroline, the sister of circus rider and manager Charles Bacon. He also took two apprentices under wing, William Armstrong and George Ross, both of whom adopted the Nixon name (Ross would later perform under his own name). This engagement with Spalding marked the first appearance of seven-year-old apprentice, William, as a featured equestrian.

The 1845 summer season found the Nixons with John T. Potter's Great Western Circus, which toured at least in New York State and Michigan. Nixon served as equestrian director; Mrs. Nixon was listed as a rider. The apprentice tads were most likely there as well, although no mention was forthcoming.

At summer's end the Nixons returned to the Bowery Amphitheatre, but left on January 28, 1846, to join Howes & Co.'s Mammoth New York Circus at Palmo's Theatre, beginning a relationship, like the one with Tryon, that was to last for the next few years. They were out with Howes' summer tour that season, and again in 1847, when James Nixon was equestrian director. W. H. Kemp, an English clown, who was to become Nixon's partner in a circus venture, was also engaged. The show went from Newark, New Jersey, on April 26th to stands in Pennsylvania, New York State, Michigan, Ohio and closing at Cumberland, Maryland, October 7th.

This pattern continued during 1848. Nixon, with his "talented children," as Odell phrased it, was again with Tryon's indoor show; then, in the spring of that year, the Nixon "family" and Kemp went out once more with the eastern unit of Howes & Co. The season began with a two-week stand in Brooklyn and continued into New Jersey, Pennsylvania, New York State, Ohio, and Kentucky until the end of October.

In 1848 a New Broadway Circus opened in an arena near Spring Street under the proprietorship of Tryon and Corporal Thompson, on grounds which had been used for years by circuses and other itinerant showmen because of the proximity to Niblo's Garden. A large and airy pavilion was erected, with circular galleries forming a spacious and comfortable auditorium and with a narrow entryway situated between Broadway and Niblo's saloon, the whole of which was given the title of "Alhambra."

James Nixon was a member of this company and, according to Odell, served as an "elegant" ringmaster. The Alhambra opened in October and, as Tom Picton put it, "flickered for a brief season and then ignominiously departed."[121] the circus having fled, the Alhambra was converted into the galleries of the International Art Union.

A daughter, Adelaide, was born in New York City this year. She was to make her first appearance on stage as a vocalist at Butler's Music Hall, 444 Broadway, New York City, in 1864. Sickness caused her to take leave from entertaining for a while; but when she resumed her professional activity she appeared in New Orleans at the Academy of Music for Spalding, Rogers & Bidwell's company; and that winter of 1865-66 in

---

121. Col. Tom Picton (edited by William L. Slout), *Old Gotham Theatricals*, p. 25-26.

Havana, Cuba, at Chiarini's circus. While there she received instructions as an equestrienne and, before leaving the eight-month engagement, could ride a principal act.

For the 1848 summer season, the Nixons were connected with the western unit of Howes & Co.'s Great United States Circus, Nixon again serving as equestrian director. Kemp, like an unshakable shadow, was with the company as well. After opening in Brooklyn on March 27th with a combined roster of both units, the route took the show through New Jersey, Pennsylvania, New York State, Ohio, Kentucky, Indiana, and back to Pennsylvania for an October 27th closing. At winter quarters in Pittsburgh the outfit was sold to John P. Crane on November 22nd.

It is in the year of 1849 when Nixon began his climb into the managerial saddle. The show which Howes had sold to Crane was renamed Crane & Co.'s Great Oriental Circus and went out the following season with Nixon as its manager. The "Oriental" in the title, Thayer tells us, referred to the dragon chariot drawn by a team of ten camels. The advertisements informed us that "The establishment on entering town will be preceded by the Monster Dragon Chariot, drawn by Ten Camels of the Syrian breed, lately imported from the Deserts of Arabia for Crane & Company." It was further announced that 40 carriages were required to convey the performers and musicians from town to town. There was also a Fairy Chariot drawn by 12 diminutive ponies, none over 36 inches in height, driven by Master William Nixon. James Nixon was prominent on the program, assisted by two pupils, George and Albert; Madame Camilla Gardner was the star equestrienne, with her riding clowned by W. H. Kemp; Dan Gardner was the comic singing clown; Louis J. Lipman, the scenic rider; William Smith, the two-horse rider; Samuel Lee, featured juggler and performer of cannonball feats. The Wells family was also aboard, with Miss Louisa Wells as the artistic *danseuse*. The closing number of the show was a set of miniature hippodrome races, put on entirely with ponies and juvenile equestrians, a sort of burlesque sporting scene entitled "The Pony Races."[122]

Then, according to Odell, on December 3rd, Nixon and family joined the New Manhattan Circus, located in New York City on Grand Street at the East River near the Williamsburgh Ferry. The establishment, which had begun operations around the middle of November, did not last long, situated as it was "so near the seat of the old Mount Pitt Circus and of the recent Neighborhood Playhouse."[123]

The Nixon bunch joined the James M. June & Co. Circus (with S. B. Howes as a partner) for the 1850 season. The show opened in New York City on April 21st, after which it undertook a lengthy tour through the eastern states, then Pennsylvania and Maryland, terminating in Baltimore on October 2nd, where it settled into winter quarters. William F. Wallett, the

---

122. Charles Bernard, *Billboard*, December 31, 1932, p. 64, 77.

123. George C. D. Odell, *Annals of the New York Stage*, Vol. V, p. 578.

English clown, and the equestrian Tourniaire family were featured. Kemp was there, too. The outdoor paraphernalia put to bed, James M. June & Co. moved into the Bowery Amphitheatre, where it opened October 28th with much of the summer roster, including the Nixons, and remained past mid-April.

We lose a clear track of Nixon following this engagement. There were two units of June & Co. on the road for the summer of 1851, but there is no evidence that he was with either. He comes in view again on December 23rd, however, when he was advertised on the bill of Welch's National Circus, Philadelphia. In the summer season of 1852, we find him still with Welch, performing the duties of equestrian director for one of the two units the General put out, Welch's National Circus and Histrionic Arena. The show, managed by George Russell, opened in Philadelphia in March before touring in New York State, Pennsylvania, and New England. William F. Wallett was principal clown; Levi J. North, principal rider. North also worked Tammany, his performing horse. Caroline Nixon was listed as working a pony act of some kind. Other Nixon names on the roster were Albert, George, and Jean. Whatever happened to William? Thayer has listed him with J. M. June & Co., suggesting that his apprenticeship had terminated at this time. A bill for Rufus Welch's 1853 winter circus, the National Circus and Theatre, which occupied the site of the Continental Hotel, Philadelphia, lists Nixon as equestrian manager.[124]

---

124. Reproduced in the *Clipper*, June 24, 1876, p. 100.

With the opening of Franconi's Hippodrome, Nixon appeared there as its equestrian director. A syndicate had been formed in the winter of 1852-53 by eight showmen including Avery Smith, Seth B. Howes, Richard Sands, and Lewis B. Titus. A lot was selected on the corner of Twenty-third Street and Broadway. A two-storied, brick-walled, canvas-roofed structure was built, which housed a 700-foot track and 4,000 seats. With the idea of introducing Roman hippodrome games to the American public, the place opened on May 2, 1853. There were races of various kinds—two- and five-horse, the usual chariot, as well as ostrich, camel, elephant, and ponies ridden by monkeys; there were aerial equilibriums, performed thirty feet from the ground; and pageantries such as *The Field of the Cloth of Gold*, in which men dressed as knights presented mock battles.

Nixon was also equestrian director for the Castle Garden Circus in the fall of 1854. The place, managed by J. Vanderbilt, opened on October 23rd and ran through November 25th.[125] Following, according to T. Allston Brown, the Nixons, James, William, and George, wintered at the Philadelphia Theatre for Welch & Lent. The place opened November 1, 1854, overlapping the season at Castle Garden, and closed with a benefit for Dan Rice on April 24th. Then, what appears to be almost the entire Castle Garden roster went on the

---

125. The roster included Mme. Marin, Mrs. Smith, Mrs. Robert Ellingham, Misses Cline and Cook, Henry Madigan, Charles Davis, A. Sylvester, Harry Whitby, James Nixon, Fred Sylvester, William Lera, Tom King, Felix Carlo, James Myers, Hiram Day, Moses Lipman, Master Carlo, Charles and James Madigan, and George and William Nixon.

summer circuit of 1855 with Seth B. Howes' outfit—Howes, Myers & Madigan. The performing rosters of both included the Madigan family, James Myers, the Whitby's, the Nixons, Tom King, and Moses Lipman. Opening on April 23rd in Patterson, the show toured through New Jersey, Pennsylvania, New York State, then into Ontario, Canada, and down into Michigan, Ohio, and back into Pennsylvania and New Jersey, closing October 20th.

In February, 1856, Nixon and Myers were represented at the Old Broadway Theatre, where they furnished 24 horses for the equestran drama *Herne the Hunter*. The relationship seems to have continued into the summer season. Odell has Nixon with the Myers circus at Court and State Streets, Brooklyn, April 21st-23rd. The company, which he labeled "a feeble array," included Myers as clown, the Siegrist Brothers, Louisa Wells, Nixon, and W. W. Nichols.[126]

The long association of James M. Nixon and William H. Kemp paid off when the two joined together in 1857 and put out a show under the title of Nixon & Kemp, which toured territory in Ohio, Indiana, Illinois, and as far west as Iowa. The most memorable feature of the season was the introduction into circusdom of a steam calliope, a cumbersome instrument which Nixon had purchased from the Steam Music Company of Worcester, Massachussetts.[127] Kemp was the featured

---

126. Odell, VI, p. 510.

127. Thayer, Vol. III., p. 114, from the correspondence of Fred Dahlinger, Jr. The Nixon & Kemp roster included William H. Kemp, clown and co-proprietor; James M. Nixon, co-proprietor; Charles W. Fuller, agent;

clown and Horace Nichols the equestrian director. The show had an outdoor free attraction in Madame Louise, who walked a wire from the ground to the top of the tent; while, in concert, the calliope played outside during the ascension and then was taken into the tent where the musical machinery was displayed to a curious public.

The summer season over, Nixon went back to Tryon as equestrian director for the New National Circus, 84 Bowery, where VanAmburgh & Co.'s cages of wild animals and an equestrian troupe held forth, made up of such performing lights as Eaton and Den Stone, the Nicolo Family, Richard Hemmings, E. H. Perry, and the educated elephant Tippo Saib. In January it was announced that, for the first time in the United States, wild animals would be fed at the matinee of the 9th in full presence of the audience, the chef for the occasion being Prof. Langworthy. A pupil of Langworthy's, May Livingston, entered a den of animals for the first time on the 13th. *Cinderella* was produced on the 18th by a group of children under the supervision of Nixon. The place continued in operation, adding a variety of guest performers, through the 15th of March before the straw was swept away and the dramatic actors reappeared.

The following season, 1858, Nixon & Kemp went into Canada and then moved through the New England

---

Horace Nichols, equestrian director; Tom Linton, stilts; Bob Smith, clown; Chinese juggling troupe; Mons. DeBach, rider; Azi Cheriff, contortionist; François Siegrist, acrobat; Alonzo Hubbell, Herculean performer; Mlle. Louise, ascensionist; Mme. Kemp; Mme. DeBach; Miss Rieford.

states and into the Middle West. They were billed as two shows with ads running side by side, one proclaiming the arrival of J. M. Nixon's Great American Circus and the other of Kemp's Mammoth English Circus. The double advertisement included the following:

> "PARTICULAR NOTICE: By an arrangement effected between the proprietors of Nixon's Great American Circus and Kemp's Mammoth English Circus, the two companies will perform together under one pavilion, giving all the performances advertised by each for one single price of admission, until further notice.
> 
> "It is also agreed that the companies will travel together under the title of the "Great Anglo-American Exhibition"; that each company shall make a separate and independent procession into town, attended by their respective military bands; and that, in order to enable the two companies to give a full performance of everything announced in both bills, the gymnastic feats of each company will be given in one ring at the same time, the performers being distinguished by their several badges, as follows: the English wearing a red ribbon attached to the right shoulder, and the Americans a blue ribbon on their left shoulder."[128]

---

128. Richard E. Conover notes, Circus World Museum. Also, ads reproduced in the *Clipper*, June 24, 1876, p. 100.

The combined shows listed a highly respectable roster of performers. Australian James Melville was riding his first season in this country. Others featured included the Lake Family, equestrian Omar Richardson, three Herculean performers—Libby, Paul, and Gregoire; five clowns—Kemp, William Lake, Signor Bliss, Robert Butler, and Amelia Butler (daughter of jester John Wells, purported to be the first female clown in America). The steam-spouting music department was enhanced by the acquisition of two bands under the leadership of Ned Kendall of Nixon's' troupe and Peter Vost of Kemp's.

At the finish of the summer season, Nixon & Kemp took over the Palace Gardens, Sixth Avenue and Fourteenth Street, New York City. The Lakes remained in the company and introduced at that time a new performer in the family, billed as Mlle. Emeline Loyalle, their four-year-old equestrienne daughter, Emma Louise Lake. Tony and William Pastor and Charles Bliss were also on the bill.

Following this engagement, the Nixon and Kemp management was dissolved; at which time Kemp left performing and returned to his former occupation as a gold leaf manufacturer. Nixon & Co.'s Mammoth Circus, with James Melville taking over Kemp's half of the management, went to Boston for a stand that lasted from November 29, 1858 through January 8, 1859, before opening at New York's Niblo's Garden on January 27th with the famous clown, Dan Rice, and his trained animals as the big attraction. The run ended around the middle of April, when the summer tour began through the eastern states and Canada, featuring Dan Castello as principal clown, along with Don Juan, his educated bull.[129]

On October 3rd, Nixon brought his tented troupe back to New York City and staked out at Broadway and Thirteenth Street for a week. The company paraded with their stud of horses and other paraphernalia behind the lead of their colossal band chariot drawn by a forty-horse hitch and driven by Madame Mason, a lady of vague biography but billed as "formerly of the London and Parisian circuses." Then, on the 10th, the show property was auctioned off.

Now, free of pressing responsibilities, James Nixon, along with a Mr. Moore, the stage manager at Niblo's, went to Europe to engage artists for the approaching winter season. The recruiting trip would, within a matter of months, result in the high point of Nixon's managerial career.

January, 1860! Barely before New Year's Eve hangovers were bestilled, came the announcement of the auspicious arrival to America of William Cooke and what was advertised as Cooke's Equestrian Troupe from Astley's Royal Amphitheatre, London, soon to perform at the famous Niblo's Garden, New York City. Cooke! Astley! What a joyous sound to those familiar names and what an exciting circus tradition they repre-

---

129. Thayer, Vol. III, p. 269, lists James Melville as co-proprietor. Others in the company included Charles W. Fuller, agent; Mme. Mason, teamstress of forty-horse hitch; Tom Lenton, clown; Louise Melville, rider; Mons. Paul, Herculean performer; Caroline Nixon; W. W. Nichols, rider; Fred Rentz, clown; Signor Bliss, clown. Mons. Gregoire joined later.

sented.

William Cooke (1802?-1886) was a third generation of the famous Cooke dynasty which began in Scotland with old Thomas Cooke in the 1750s. Thomas' son, Thomas Taplin Cooke (1782-1866), a rope walker, rider and strong man, fathered somewhere between thirteen and nineteen children and still had time to establish his own circus in 1816 and operate continually until his fateful venture to America in 1836. That year he crossed the waters with a company comprised of thirty-seven of his own family, most of which performed or assisted the performers. There were thirty or forty of the finest horses ever imported into the country—some full-blooded Arabians and a number of small Burmese ponies, the latter ridden by the infant prodigies of the Cooke clan. But on the morning of February 3, 1838, at the Front Street Circus in Baltimore, Maryland, a devastating conflagration left Cooke bereft of ring stock and circus paraphernalia and eventually sent him back to England, financially depleted and emotionally embittered. After having introduced America to such spectacles as *Mazeppa* and *Alexander the Great's Entry into Babylon,* he continued to perform in them until his death at the age of eighty-four.

William, Thomas Taplin Cooke's second son, overshadowed by his younger brother James' equestrian virtues, became a clown, rope-walker and strong-man. He formed his own circus company in 1834 and eventually gave up performing to direct equestrian dramas and train ring animals. He took over the management of Astley's Amphitheatre, London, in 1853 with assets of £50,000 and laboriously managed that famous arena until his seven-year lease and much of his wealth ran out in 1859. During the length of this tenancy he had been kept afloat by his touring tented attraction; so one can only speculate that, like others before him, he came to America to enlarge his depleted treasury.

The circus with Cooke's name opened on January 16, 1860, at Niblo's Garden and, as George C. D. Odell put it, the company "took possession and startled the most blasé." The initial advertising read:

> "Cooke's Royal Amphitheatre, the extensive and brilliant equestrian troupe of Mr. William Cooke, late of Astley's Amphitheatre, now performing at Niblo's Garden every evening and on Wednesday and Saturday afternoon commencing at 2:00. The matinees on Wednesdays and Saturdays are given for the accommodation of families residing at a distance and those who prefer attending in the daytime. This splendid equestrian troupe comprises all the great living artists in the profession and the entertainments are the most original, novel and refined ever witnessed in this country. Boxes 50¢, orchestra chairs $1, private boxes $5 and $6."[130]

Niblo's Garden! This gracious old venue had its own colorful tradition. Originally the site of the old

---

130. New York *Clipper*, March 31, 1860, p. 398.

Bayard farm, located away out of town on Broadway, or what was generally known as the Albany Post Road, it became a drill ground for militia officers shortly after the War of 1812. Later, a celebrated breeder of race horses, Charles Henry Hall, secured the property and built for himself a two-storied, slate-roofed mansion of solid brick, and for his prized quadrupeds a shingled palace of wood and glass, the sum of which rested on grounds lined by an avenue of poplar trees, enlivened with decorative floribunda. Here, sometime shortly after 1823, William Niblo took memorable possession.

Niblo, "an active little man with keen, shrewd money-making eyes," was the industrious proprietor of the old Bank Coffee House, named after its neighbor, the bank administering to the financial wants of New Yorkers, located in the business quarter of downtown Gotham. There, for some years, Niblo successfully served up such gastronomic delights as turtle soup and salmon from Boston until, ambitious for greater glories, he transformed the old Bayard farm site into a summer garden spot, wherein ice creams and other delectables were served up. Amid a setting of latticed arbors, ornamented by gorgeous illuminations, and within the sound of tireless musicians, devourers of such delicacies could lounge or stroll about the Edenic grounds on torpid summer evenings, interrupted merely by such novelties as balloon ascensions and pyrotechnic displays or periodic flights of tight-rope performers. At the outset, the gardens were located far up town, a milestone from City Hall, and beyond the service of the city stage lines. Undaunted, Niblo ingeniously created his own stage line, equipped with new and innovative vehicular design.

In 1828, as the resort had grown in popularity, the training stable was converted into a concert saloon, Theatre San Souci, wherein Madame Otto warbled "Meet Me by Moonlight Alone" and Gambati launched his solos on the French horn. Then, sadly, on the morning of July 18, 1846, the little theatre was destroyed by fire. But a house with such precious memories could not be easily consigned to ashes. The place was re-built in a manner that surpassed in elegance and utility the previous structure and opened for trade on July 30, 1849; after which, the theatre housed a continuous offering of high-class performers and performances.

And now, in January of 1860, Nixon re-established himself at Niblo's Garden, taking over the proprietorship in preparation for the arrival of Cooke and a talented company. The place was specially prepared for circus performances, the ring being covered with a thick Canton matting, a decided improvement for indoor arenas, being at once a sure and elastic footing for the horses and entirely free from the dust and annoyances of the old system of tanbark and sawdust. All of the costumes and properties were tastefully selected.

And, most importantly, thanks to James Nixon, the company was a combination of outstanding English and American performers. James Robinson, premier Boston-born bareback rider, was summoned home from his European tour. He had accompanied Howes

& Cushing's Great American Circus to London in the spring of 1857 and throughout his stay established himself as a star performer in both England and on the Continent. The Hanlon Brothers, English gymnasts, were engaged[131] (they had made their American debut at Niblo's in 1858 under Nixon's management). Joe Pentland, famous for his impromptu songs and portrayal of a drunken sailor on horseback, was the feature clown. Sallie Stickney, billed as Mlle. Heloise, performed her equestrienne act of leaping, cutting, pirouetting, and one-foot riding, showing a beauty in face and form which was to rank her at the top of her profession. There were also William Duverney, the "greatest dislocationist in existence"; Mons. F. DeBach, Parisian equestrian and juggler on horseback (who had only recently performed at Metropolitan Garden, Second Avenue and Thirteenth Street); and a Mr. Charlton, billed as the "oldest of gymnasts."

Mlle. Heloise! Why Mlle. Heloise, you may ask? Well, the answer was forthcoming in a letter to the *Clipper* dated March 13, 1860, from her father, S. P. Stickney:

> "I noticed in the *Clipper* of March 10th that a correspondent asks the question why Miss Sallie Stickney should drop her own name and

---

[131]. *The Spirit of the Times* referred to six Hanlon brothers. They would have been Thomas (1836-1868), George (1840-1926), William (1842-1923), Alfred (1844-1886), Edward (1846-1931), and Frederick (b. 1848). Thayer suggests that only three were engaged. We know George and Thomas were there. William did not join at this time due to an injury, but may have been added some months later.

assume that of 'Heloise.' I will answer. When Miss Stickney arrived in New York this winter to fulfill an engagement at Niblo's, Mr. Nixon desired her to use her name 'Eloise,' the name she used when she appeared at the same house under Rufus Welch's management in the winter of 1851. Through an error on the part of the person who made out the bill, instead of 'Eloise,' her name was printed 'Heloise,' and it was not considered of sufficient importance to make the correction. Her real name is Sallie Eloise Stickney."[132]

The observer for the New York *Times* found the opening performance "in the highest degree satisfactory," an achievement which elicited abundant applause from one of the most crowded houses he had ever witnessed. He was impressed with the riding of the leading equestrians; for, as he expressed it, "in New York, as in every other city of the Union, good circus riding is thoroughly understood and appreciated." He went on to state that "Mlle. Ella Zoyara, the principal lady of the company, is a very remarkable performer, and the graceful daring of her 'acts' brought down the heartiest applause of the house."

Thomas Hanlon's *l'échelle périleuse* was found

---

132. New York *Clipper*, March 24, 1860, p. 390. The explanation came in a letter from Boston dated March 13th. The 1851 engagement at Niblo's for manager Rufus Welch occurred from April 4th to the 26th under the guise of Cirque Français. In the troupe with Mlle. Eloise were Mr. Lee, Mlle. Caroline Loyale, François Loisset, C. Rivers, Richards, Master Derious, Eaton Stone, etc.

to be stimulating and unique. After going through a sequence of gyrations on a swing attached to the ceiling at one end of the proscenium, the gymnast suddenly released himself from it and, flying some twenty or thirty feet through the air, grabbed onto a rope on the other side. "The feat is terrible to behold, but beautifully performed."[133]

A representative for the New York *Clipper* was on hand for the opening as well; however, at first glance, he was not as impressed as his colleague from the *Times*. But, returning the following week, he found decided improvements which were passed off to the entire satisfaction of a numerous and highly respectable assemblage. It is with gratitude to him that we are able to disclose the evening's program.

As the curtain rose, a very attractive scene was at once presented to view, the entire troupe appearing on the stage in the various characters representing the exercises of a Chinese festival—a procession of lanterns, the feats of a troupe of acrobats, the tricks of several conjurers with knives, balls, plates, etc., and finally a series of ballet dances (the corps of dancers being somewhat meager), all this along with equestrian exercises in the ring. The closing part of this opening spectacle presented a very attractive *tout ensemble*, the very appropriate music of the efficient orchestra being a marked feature to the piece. The next thing in order was an exhibition of the equestrian talents of Mlle. Heloise, termed an "act of beauty," which was judged

---

133. New York *Times*, January 17, 1860, p. 5.

an exceedingly graceful and beautiful performance. The comic act of Mr. Charlton on stilts was next on the program. The *Clipper* observer found the powers of equilibrium possessed by this artist, especially in the drunken scene, at once surprising and amusing to the extreme. This was followed by the exercises of a couple of diminutive ponies whose equine intellects had been cultivated by Mr. Cooke. A globe performance on horseback by Mons. DeBach followed that of the ponies. Next, considered by our man a great feature, was the "truly wonderful and perilous feats of agility and strength" exhibited by Thomas Hanlon on the aerial apparatus attached to the proscenium of the theatre. Then there were Japanese games by a troupe of acrobats which afforded an amusing relief to the previous act of peril. The first part of the program closed with Master Barclay's spirited exhibition of the dangers of English hurdle racing.

After a brief intermission, the audience was introduced to the act entitled *La Corde Volante* in which Mr. Ward went through some exercises on the slack rope, concluding with throwing himself groundward with a rope around his neck. Next came the equestrian feats of Mlle. Zoyara. The *Clipper*-ite described the performance in the following manner: "...Her fine physique, which her ethereal costume fully exhibits, at once attracts the attention of the masculine gender. However, her really surprising performances draw forth repeated outbursts of applause and the occasional failures attendant upon her daring attempts, though it mars somewhat the beauty of the performance, considerably enhances the excitement, the whole series of feats being decidedly of the dangerous order...."

Then came Duverney, the contortionist, "whose astonishing postures showed what a degree of elasticity the human body is capable of by early and constant training." The twin ponies were next brought forward and their behavior afforded additional testimony of Cooke's powers over animals. The succeeding feat was termed a novel and double act *par terre* by Thomas and George Hanlon, considered a beautiful and astonishing performance and something never before witnessed on this side of the Atlantic. Their great muscular strength and their lithe and agile movements, together with the grace and ease with which they performed each exercise, marked the whole exhibition one of unequaled excellence and merit. The brothers were considered "the trump cards of the troupe." James Robinson next appeared and went through a series of equestrian feats, prominent among which was his turning somersaults over flags while on horseback. In this, the *Clipper*'s man believed him to be unequaled; still, his riding on the bare back of a horse was rated as inferior to that exhibited by the Australian Melville.

The entertainment concluded with the usual equestrian comedy. Joe Pentland's wit and humor and smartness at repartee "served materially to enhance the attractive character of the whole entertainment." Some members of the audience were scolded for leaving the theatre before the last piece was commenced. "This custom is a disgrace to all who are guilty of it," the *Clipper* readers were admonished, "evincing as it does the possession of gross selfishness and want of common decency of behavior."[134]

The lollipop of the evening, taking the spotlight and making a New York debut, was decidedly Mlle. Ella Zoyara, whom Nixon had enticed from England with the offer of $500 a week, free passage for self and two servants, all medical bills, and use of a horse and carriage when required. The rider's beauty and grace upon the back of a horse at once aroused an impressive response of adulation from the Niblo patrons.

But within a few weeks the charade was challenged and the truth emerged. Ella Zoyara was in reality Omar Samuel Kingsley, a Creole from Louisiana. While a circus managed by Spencer Q. Stokes and Signor Louis Germani was playing in New Orleans, the boy was apprenticed to them by his parents at seven years of age. His Christian name is unknown but everyone called him "Sam" or "Little Sam." By the time he was eleven he showed amazing skills as a rider. Because of his physical beauty, Stokes dressed him in complete female attire, which was worn in and out of the ring. It has been stated that, once donning the clothing of a girl, he did not wear male britches again until he was nineteen. Caution was taken that his playmates were only girls his own age, developing in him the manners and grace of the female sex. Stokes' deception continued for eight years, the secret being sustained even to members

---

134. New York *Clipper*, January 28, 1860, p. 326.

of the companies in which Zoyara performed. In 1851, with Stokes as mentor, he sailed for England and a tour of the Continent, performing under the name of Ella and under the guise of a female rider. Story has it that while in Moscow a Russian count fell madly in love with him and men of nobility in the countries he visited flocked around him and bestowed unto him rich gifts. As described by a contemporary, he had "a faultless complexion of the fairest brunette type, his face never showing the slightest trace of a beard, and his features were perfect and of a most delicate, womanly character, as were also his hands and feet; his hair of raven blackness hung in luxuriant masses almost to his waist."[135]

The young man had created quite a stir before the question of his sex arose; then the stir became a storm. Once discovered, there was resentment by the press, unhappy as they were at being hoodwinked. "If the person is a man, the humbug is a very dishonest one; if a woman, for the sake of all parties, the point should be settled."[136] It was conceded that Zoyara's novelty as a rider had lost its charm; and the public, particularly the male section, many of whom had sent the boy bouquets and tender notes and other expressions of adoration, were disillusioned. Before the reality of his sex was established and while the question was yet in doubt, it was suggested that a committee of "strong-minded" women be selected to "wait upon" him and look into

---

135. Will S. Heck, "Chats With an Old Circus Man," *Billboard*, March 21, 1908, pp. 45, 48.

136. *Spirit of the Times*, February 11, 1860, p. 12.

the facts of the case; but, understandably, Zoyara was not inclined to be examined. It mattered little, for in no time the truth was out and the whole secret exposed. "Humbug is the order of the day and he who is the cleverest at imposing upon his fellows is sure to draw the dollars," wrote an irate journalist.[137] "If this person is a boy as represented, then a most bare-faced imposition has been practiced upon the American public by the management of the concern and the sooner the public resent the fraud the better," wrote yet another.[138]

Poor Cooke. He was the titular proprietor and the recipient of some of the wrath, even though he had nothing to do with the deception. "Mr. Cooke is a stranger and we fear has put too much faith in Barnum's book," wrote a *Spirit of the Times* correspondent.[139] But Nixon, seeing the publicity value at hand, included some of these quotations in his advertising, thus, in a manner, endorsing the truth of the fraud:

> "...With the exposition of one deception, the patrons of such entertainments naturally begin to inquire whether the entire concern is not an imposition. It was announced as Cooke's company from Astley's Amphitheatre, London. We have been given to understand that such is not the fact—that with the exception of the Hanlon Brothers, Zoyara, and one or two others, the company is composed of Americans, many of

---

137. New York *Clipper*, February 11, 1860, p. 342.

138. New York *Clipper*, February 4, 1860, p. 334.

139. *Spirit of the Times*, February 11, 1860, p. 12.

them engaged in New York, Philadelphia and elsewhere throughout the country.... We have heard rumors of the deceptive character of Cooke's circus ever since their opening night; but, as we judged they might have emanated from those envious of their success, we gave little credit to such reports. But, however, a color of truth given to them by the management of the concern actually advertising the Zoyara exposition, we naturally came to the conclusion that where there is so much smoke there must be some fire. We therefore respectfully ask the cooperation of our friends to place the real facts before the public as to the character of the circus and those who compose the company. Any truthful evidence on the subject will be thankfully received and honestly made use of...."[140]

Stuart Thayer tells us that Nixon paid two round-trip passages from England and back for William Cooke and his wife and a $500 weekly salary. For this, Cooke worked two liberty acts and performed the duties of equestrian manager. The circus program had an array of European ring horses and ponies, including the highly trained war horse, Emperor; the Shetland pony, Robin Grey; twin ponies, Cupid and Diamond; and the elfin pony, Will o' the Wisp, billed as the smallest equine in existence. Were these Cooke's animals? And surely, given his background, he had a hand in

---
140. New York *Clipper*, February 4, 1860, p. 334.

the staging of the equestrian spectacles. But whatever his contributions to stage and ring, his most important asset was in supplying the use of the Cooke name, a name synonymous with circus and one carried by talented members of the Cooke clan working in America at this time. Nixon made full use of it in his publicity, presenting the circus at Niblo's Garden as Cooke's Royal Circus from Astley's, when indeed, as we are aware, it wasn't Cooke's company at all but a group of independent contractors. Later, when Nixon took to the road between Niblo engagements, he was inconsistent in the use of the troupe designation, billing at various places as Nixon's Equestrian Troupe or as Cooke's Royal Circus, even though Cooke had returned to England by this time.[141]

Attendance had slackened somewhat from the crashing business at the beginning but the Zoyara controversy fanned public enthusiasm and shortly the circus was playing to large houses once again. "The circus 'draws like a horse' at Niblo's," it was observed, "and as the season is near its close, if you wish a seat lower than the ceiling, it is necessary to go early."[142] Charlton's stilt routine still drew wonderment as to how he was able to keep his equilibrium for such a length of time. Also, Duverney's act was holding up well. He had introduced the feat of resting his head on a platform while taking a complete walk around it without apparently moving it from its original posi-

---

141. Thayer, *op. cit.*, p. 115.

142. *Spirit of the Times*, February 25, 1860, p. 36.

tion. An observer felt that the performer "must be all gristle." During the run, new features were added to the program—morris dances, May poles, jugglers, and steeplechases. The season ended with the ring performance of *The Field of the Cloth of Gold* on March 3rd: "...The immense number of people who have for weeks past filled every available position, sitting or standing, has been astonishing, particularly when we know that in all entertainments of this kind but little novelty can be produced. Unquestionably, taken all and all, this thoroughly complete circus is the best that has ever been seen in the United States...."[143]

James M. Nixon was a busy man throughout the year of 1860. In addition to his involvement with the so-called Cooke circus troupe, and the soon to be installed California Menagerie, he was the house proprietor at Niblo's, where between circus visits he was still responsible for keeping the place going—booking burlesques, vaudevilles and comediettas, as well as operating the gardens with its rainbow of finely decorated flowers, spacious and magnificent arbors and botanical and aquaria exhibits. Also, it was at this time that Nixon had the great American actor, Edwin Forrest, under a one-hundred night contract to perform in the principal cities of the country. But, the year still young, the industrious Nixon was not ready to retire just yet.

The so-called Cooke's Equestrian Troupe, terminated its run at Niblo's Garden on March 3, 1860, and

---

143. *Spirit of the Times*, March 3, 1860, p. 40.

moved to the Boston Academy of Music (formerly Boston Theatre). The troupe had drawn well and could have remained in place and enjoyed respectable business. Nevertheless, the horses and acrobats gave way to Mr. and Mrs. Barney Williams, who opened at the Garden of Niblo on March 5th in a new piece called *Patience and Perseverance*. It was a return engagement, the couple having performed there to crowded houses the previous October and November.

Cooke's Circus opened at the Boston theatre, also on the 5th of March, to what was near a house record. Mlle. Zoyara, still being the attraction, caught bouquets tossed from the audience. But after the opening week the houses began to slack off, the Bostonians showing more restraint than their New York cousins. Also, the original levels of admission were found to be too "pricey" for the general public, so a reduction was soon made. And, after all, only across the way the Morris Bros., Pell & Trowbridge Minstrels were offering a new burlesque with the alluring title of *Macbeth, or, the Downfall of Gilson's Beanery*.

After five weeks in Boston, Nixon's circus took back Niblo's on April 9th with Ella Zoyara, James Robinson, the Hanlons, Joe Pentland and company—Cooke having departed—and began offering a series of spectacles. A new version of *The Bronze Horse*, with musical and dramatic features and an equine ascension as a grand climax, was produced in April and extremely well received. There followed *Merry Sports of England* and *Blue Beard*, the latter being cleverly mounted and featuring the singing of Miss Marian Macarthy, who had joined Nixon's company in early May. The troupe was also enhanced at this time by a renowned Italian equestrian, Signor Sebastian Quaglieni, who performed Pickwickian impersonations on horseback. Although the houses continued to be well-filled, the engagement terminated on May 26th with *Cinderella*, a spectacle enacted almost entirely by children.[144]

After leaving Niblo's Garden at the end of May, Nixon's circus went on tour. There were short stays in Brooklyn, Newark, and Philadelphia, and then the company visited towns in Pennsylvania.[145] During this time the epithet of Old Grizzly Adams and his California Menagerie was added to the Nixon calendar, the result of Nixon entering into a joint arrangement with P. T. Barnum and J. C. Adams for exhibiting Adams' animals.

It had been rumored in February that Barnum was negotiating for a share of Old Grizzly Adams' California Menagerie, which was then en route from

---

144. Other members of the troupe included E. Rivers, Foster, Nagel, Davenport, Ruggles, Ellingham, Andrews, Cooke, Whitby, DeBach, Stickney, Mrs. Rynar, and Mrs. Nixon. William Hanlon was also scheduled to join his brothers but his appearance was delayed. He had been unable to perform because of an injury sustained some months earlier. Usually billed as Signor Sebastion, Quaglieni (d. 1882) performed in America for about 25 years and was considered excellent in somersault and carrying acts and as a bareback rider. He had just closed an engagement with Dockrill & Leon, Iron Amphitheatre, Havana, when he was stricken with yellow fever and died. His son, Romeo Sebastian, was a circus rider.

145. The New York *Clipper*, September 1, 1860, p. 159, suggests that the show went as far west as St. Paul, Minnesota; but Stuart Thayer told me that Orton & Older sometimes used the Cooke title in the West in 1860 and they were in St. Paul.

San Francisco. Actually, Barnum purchased a half-interest in it from a man who had preceded Adams' arrival. On hearing of this, the California menagerie owner claimed that the man had only advanced him money and had no right to sell a share of the exhibition; but he ultimately consented to the arrangement, figuring the experienced Barnum could more ably manage his New York engagement.

James Capen "Grizzly" Adams, California hunter and trapper and exhibitor of wild beasts, was born in Medway, Massachusetts. When the gold rush fever struck, he migrated to California, ultimately moving into the mountains to live. At some point, he killed a female bear, then captured and trained her two cubs. He acquired other animals native to the region and began a menagerie collection. The bears were trained to walk on their hind legs, talk on cue, wrestle, etc. A nasty encounter with one in the Sierra Nevadas in 1855 resulted in his sustaining severe wounds to the head and neck, leaving an indentation in his skull the size of a silver dollar. Shortly after that incident, he moved out of the mountains and began exhibiting his collection, first in San Jose and then San Francisco. In 1856 he entered the circus business with Joseph Rowe, until Rowe left with his troupe of performers for Hawaii. Before moving his menagerie east, Adams again had an encounter with one of his bears, which opened the injury on his skull, exposing a portion of his brain. Then upon leaving San Francisco on February 11th, Adams and his cornucopia of animals endured a

100-day voyage before arriving in New York harbor. The 19 cages, most measuring 10' x 4' x 4', housed the pack of beasts during the arduous passage.

Barnum and Nixon erected a tent at Broadway and Thirteenth Street in which to house the menagerie; and on opening day, April 30th, a blaring band paraded the animal cages down Broadway and up the Bowery with old Adams on a platform wagon in his hunting togs, mounted atop the largest of three grizzlies. Within the tent were displayed several wolves, a half-dozen different species of California bears, California lions, buffalo, elk, twenty or thirty large grizzly bears, and "Old Neptune," a sea lion from the Pacific Ocean;[146] all this and Adams' trained grizzlies demonstrating their agility and versatility through singing, climbing, dancing, vaulting, and somersaulting.

With horses and riders gone, the Niblo's Garden theatre underwent refurbishing for a summer re-opening on June 4th. Nixon's advertisements announced the arrival of such featured entertainers as the Nelson Sisters, plump Polly Marshall, and the Hanlon Brothers. Niblo's Saloon was also opened for summer frivolities under the Nixon management.

The California Menagerie continued to exhibit at Broadway and Thirteenth Street until July 7th. Then, after a doctor's suggestion that injuries would soon cause his death, and wishing to leave his wife with financial security, Grizzly Adams sold his share of the menagerie establishment to Barnum, who then

---

146. P. T. Barnum, *Struggles and Triumphs; or Forty Years' Recollections,* p. 530-38.

combined with James M. Nixon to take Cooke's Royal Circus with Old Grizzly Adams' California Menagerie on tour. Adams struck a deal to go along for ten weeks at a total salary of $500. After fulfilling most of the contract, he left and retired to his daughter's home in Neponset, Massachusetts, where he died a short time later.

The dramatic season at Niblo's did not go well with the public and thus ended on June 28th. The equestrian troupe, after completing their summer tour, what the *Spirit of the Times* called "one of the most successful campaigns to the principal towns, cities, and villages of the West ever achieved by a traveling company," moved back in on Monday, July 30th. Nixon's bills, labeled by the *Spirit* writer as "something 'stunning' in their lengthened sweetness long drawn out," heralded the arrival of Mlle. Zoyara, the Hanlon Brothers, James Robinson, Duverney, Charlton, DeBach, Quaglieni, and Pentland, with "forty auxiliaries, each of brilliant talent," all opening for a short season. The company was greeted with enthusiastic applause as each artist respectively appeared before the audience. "The performances were of the same varied, exciting, and excellent description as already have placed Mr. Nixon at the head of the managerial and equestrian profession."[147] What was called an historical pageant, *The Oriental Festival*, was restored to the Niblo stage; also the equestrian spectacle, *The Shield of the Cloth of Gold*, presented in tandem with *The Steeple-Chase;*

---

147. *Spirit of the Times*, August 11, 1860, p. 328.

*or Life in Merry England*, which was enhanced by the importation of six thoroughbred horses from the British Isles. The advertisement promised that all this would be produced in rapid succession, with original music composed by John Cooke (another Cooke?), leader of the orchestra. Although the arenic action was impaired this time from lack of space, the ring being smaller than in the earlier stand, the houses were filled with "country cousins" and other summer visitors to the city. By the first of September, Nixon was including amateur gymnastic contests to the program in which "30 gentlemen" participated. This prompted an explanation in the advertising two days later: "The management having witnessed the gratification evinced by the citizens of and strangers to New York in the progression of physical education on the part of the students of healthy pastimes, their rising generation of the metropolis, has yielded to the request of many well-known citizens, and concluded to continue the exercises one week longer, permitting any amateur of respectability to enter the lists, thus affording an opportunity for friendly emulation among the New York gymnasts; and allowing their fathers, mothers, sisters, and wives a fair chance to see their proficiency in active science."

Certainly the fathers, mothers, sisters, and wives of the amateur contestants would help swell the coffers of the circus treasury. But this was just filler until the run came to a close on Friday, September 14th, and the stables vacated to make way for a two-hundred night tenancy of the great Edwin Forrest, who opened his stay with *Hamlet* on the 17th. In anticipation, at 3:30 p.m. on the 12th, an auction was held in the theatre vestibule with the sale of orchestra chairs and private boxes for Forrest's opening night.[148] Nixon was beginning to Barnumize.

The tour of the California Menagerie through the New England States began around August 4th. Performing variously under the titles of Cooke's Royal Circus, Nixon & Adams, and Cooke & Adams, the show moved through Rhode Island, Massachusetts, and New Hampshire until the end of September. After which, Nixon sold the equipment to Boston showman George K. Goodwin and put out an outfit on rails under the name of Nixon's Royal Circus, which was routed through the southern states—Virginia, North Carolina, South Carolina, Georgia, Alabama—and then opened a stand in New Orleans.[149] It is assumed that the company utilized the local rail systems for a good portion of these travels.

The idea of transporting show equipment by rail was just beginning to catch hold. The decade of the 1850s was called the most dynamic period in the history of American railroads, as railroad building reflected the optimism, expansion, and prosperity of

---

148. New York *Times*, July 30-September 14.

149. Thayer, *op. cit.*, p. 116, 270. The roster included Levi J. North, rider; Herr Cline, rope dancer; Mons. DuBuch; Hazlett; Kincaide; A. Levy; William Naylor; Bob Smith, clown; Whitney & Burrows; Frank Whittaker; Masters Bogart, Coyle, G. North, H. North, Willie, Frank and John Whittaker; and the trick horse, Spot Beauty, and dancing horse, Tammy. The Whitby and Whittaker families departed toward the end of the season to perform at Carmac Woods, Philadelphia.

that era. By 1860 track mileage within the states east of the Mississippi totaled around 30,000. But full use of rail at this time was inhibited by a variance in gauge size from one rail line to another. Circuses moving on cars designed to operate on the standard gauge (4'-8½" track-width) had to unload and transfer equipment to cars compatible with, say, the southern gauge (5' track-width), these two sizes being the most popular in use. Nevertheless, in 1853 Charles H. Castle and H. M. Whitbeck originated a circus out of Cincinnati designed to travel by steamboat, canal, and railroad. In 1856 Spalding & Rogers' New Railroad Circus went on the road with all appurtenances being carried by rail and specifically constructed so they could be used on any gauge size. And by 1859 there were several shows out whose title boldly implied "Railroad Circus."

Stuart Thayer's routing for Nixon's Royal Circus begins at the nation's capital, a direct line on standard gauge track from Philadelphia and Baltimore, and continues to Richmond, Norfolk, Petersburg, Weldon, Raleigh, Goldsboro, Wilmington, Charleston, Savannah, Macon, Columbus, Montgomery, and finally New Orleans. Following Nixon's movement through the process of full-blown speculation, the circus could have jumped to Richmond on standard gauge; taken standard and southern gauge, or boat travel, to Norfolk; then southern gauge to Petersburg. Weldon, North Carolina, a much smaller community, must have been a jump-breaker to Raleigh, both being on standard gauge. The same gauge could move the troupe to

Goldsboro, intersecting with another standard gauge to Wilmington. From there the road to Charleston, South Carolina, was fitted with the southern gauge, which continued into Georgia for the Savannah, Macon and Columbus dates. We are now on the Georgia-Alabama border and must use a standard gauge to get to Montgomery, the end of the line before reaching New Orleans. Here we find ourselves in a quandary. We can either take a senseless, round-about rail route to the Crescent City or move directly south on a southern gauge rail to Pensacola, Florida, and thence by boat to New Orleans. The latter appears the most logical. In any case, primary rail travel was not only feasible for the Nixon entourage but, by all accounts, preferable. Five days after leaving Montgomery, the circus opened on Saturday, November 19th, at the St. Charles Theatre, New Orleans.

Nixon's Royal Circus remained at this stand for three weeks, closing on Friday, December 8th. Two days later the show opened in Havana, Cuba, at the Villanueva Theatre for the winter season, the Hanlon Brothers and Ella Zoyara still the feature attractions. Back home the breezes of national anxiety were accelerating. Only ten more days would pass before South Carolina seceded from the Union.

Elements of James M. Nixon's circus arrived in New York City from Havana on March 23, 1861, and opened at Niblo's Garden on the 28th where, in combination with the Ronzani ballet, the troupe filled out the remaining off nights until the end of the theatre season. Ella Zoyara and Mlle. Heloise were augmented by bareback rider Quaglieni; rider and leaper Tom King; rider and acrobat William Kincade; and other American performers whom the creative Nixon presented under Spanish names. A repeated spectacle of *Cinderella* with a cast of seventy-five children was a companion attraction. On April 27th Nixon took a well deserved benefit. The theatre closed its doors two days later, an occasion that ended Nixon's management of Niblo's Garden. War prevailing, this grand old house would remain dark for a period of eight months.

At the end of their engagement, the remaining contingent of Nixon's circus company left St. Jago de Cuba on March 24th on the *Black Squall* (H. W. King, Captain; Welch & Brothers, owners) to return to the mainland. Alas! After a stormy sixteen days, the ship was wrecked near Cape Hatteras, on April 19, 1861, with a total destruction to the vessel and cargo. Two performers, William Nixon, the adopted son of James M., and one of the crew were drowned. All horses except one and all property and wardrobe were lost. Nothing was covered by insurance.[150]

\* \* \* \* \* \* \*

Neither the war nor the wreck of the *Black Squall* deterred James M. Nixon. For the tenting season of

---

150. New York *Clipper*, May 11, 1861, p. 31. George Ross, equestrian, and Wessell T. B. VanOrden, advertiser, suffered broken legs from the falling of a boom, which forced them to stay behind when the company continued homeward. On their recovery they boarded the steamer *State of Georgia* at Fort Monroe and arrived in New York City on June 2nd.

1861, Sloat's New York Circus combined with Nixon's Royal Circus to form the First National Union Circus, advertising as "adapted to the exigencies of war." The "Car of Freedom," which led the parade, was drawn by ten horses under the rein of Madame Mason, clothed to resemble the Goddess of Liberty; and atop the car was a military band dressed in the familiar uniforms of Zouaves. The list of performers included Le Jeune Burt, Signor Sebastian, the Nelson Brothers, the southern clown Sam Long, and Ella Zoyara. Zoyara's mentor, Spencer Q. Stokes, was there as equestrian director, with his thoroughbred war horse, General Scott.[151] The show, which performed primarily in New Jersey and the New England states throughout the summer, moved onto the traditional South Fifth Street lot in Williamsburg in August before the tent was transported to New York City and pitched on the open grounds between the Palace Gardens concert pavilion and the Fourteenth Street Theatre, Fourteenth and Broadway.

The circus opened there on September 2, 1861, for an indefinite stay and remained until the scorn of fall weather pronounced the season's end. During the run, Grizzly Adams' bears performed their amazing acrobatics, Joe Pentland reappeared as clown, and Eaton Stone was there with his buffalos driven in harness. Signor Zoyara, now of the male gender, the same Zoyara who had previously created such controversy at Niblo's the year before, drew the journalistic comment,

---

151. Bernard, *Billboard*, October 27, 1934, p. 40.

"We must say, however, that Zoyara makes a much better looking woman than man."[152] But the rider did not abandon the skirt for tights exclusively; later in the run he performed as he had for the public on his New York debut, dressed in the feminine frills of Mlle. Ella Zoyara.

Edwin Forrest was apparently still working under the Nixon ringmaster's whip. M. B. Leavitt, who called Nixon "the most enterprising showman I knew well in the Sixties," tells us Nixon opened the Boston Theatre season of 1861-62 with the great tragedian. Forrest appeared four nights a week alongside a fine company that included John McCullough.[153]

In the spring of 1862, Nixon took a lease on Palace Gardens. The resort was first opened on July 1, 1858, as a summer promenade by DeForrest & Teesdale, where musical concerts and other exhibitions were presented. Nixon proposed converting and enlarging it into a place of Elysian beauty similar to the Cremorne Gardens of London. He developed three new features on the property—a stretch of canvas under which equestrian performances were given; a building devoted to the display of trees, flowers and shrubbery called Floral Hall; and a concert pagoda designated the Palace of Music; in all, an intermingling of natural beauty, ballet, opera, and circus.

The American Cremorne Gardens opened its doors to the public on June 9th under the business manage-

---

152. New York *Clipper*, September 14, 1861, p. 174.

153. M. B. Leavitt, *Fifty Years in Theatrical Management*, p. 64.

ment of Col. T. Allston Brown. With a recent ruckus over the concert saloon issue in the state legislature, making it illegal for a place of entertainment to sell intoxicating beverages, the management clearly announced that "no vinous, malt or spirituous liquors will be furnished or tolerated."[154] The usual evening began at 7:30 with a 1½-hour musical; that is, ballet, concert, or opera, with a change of program weekly. Patrons could stroll about the grounds while listening to such artists as Carlotta Patti, Sig. Sbriglia, and Mme. Amelia Patti-Strakosch, or an orchestra led by Harvey Dodworth. After the music was terminated, equestrian exhibitions of another 1½-hour duration were performed. Nixon's circus artists included the French equestrienne, Madame Louise Tourniaire; the Conrad Brothers, Charles and William, clowns and gymnasts; the clown Julian Kent; and Horace F. Nichols, the veteran rider, equestrian director, and ringmaster. The expected summer garden food fare was available, ices, creams, jellies, confectionery, cakes, fruits, etc. Commodore Foote and Colonel Small appeared in their elaborate chariot drawn by Lilliputian ponies to welcome the patrons. Some Iroquois Indians gave exhibitions of tribal dancing. Thomas Baker, of Laura Keene's Theatre, led the promenade orchestra. The pantomimes *Spirit of the Flood*, *The Golden Egg*, and *The Wizard Skiff* were presented in turn. Firework displays were frequently given at the close of the evening. Admission for all was 25¢; reserved armchairs

---

154. Odell, Vol. VII, p. 443.

in the Palace of Music, 25¢ extra; orchestra armchairs, 25¢ extra.

One of the features of the summer, "the chief joy of the Cremorne," was the beautiful Spanish pantomimist and *danseuse*, Isabel Cubas. Cubas was born in Valencia del Cid, Spain, in 1837 and came to America in 1861. In September of that year she appeared at New York's Winter Garden, where she attracted public notice as a fascinating and voluptuous dancer. She was under Nixon's management and had, it was said, been recently married to him; which was untrue, of course, since he was still married to his wife, Caroline, at this time. For Cubas' benefit on October 6th, she performed in J. T. Haines' time-worn piece, *The French Spy*.

The garden was shut down at the approach of cold weather. It had been a noble effort by the tireless proprietor but the outcome was a weak imitation of the English original. The season at the Cremorne did not live up to the flourish of printers' ink advertising the opening. Nixon had assembled a company of artists from the world of music and dance, which were intermixed with the more commonly appealing artists of the arena, a little something for everyone. But the novelties were not of a high order and the artists already too familiar to the New York public. The admission price was reasonable, it is true; but the prices for refreshments were far too high for a broad portion of the promenaders. At the outset, bad weather kept people away; with better weather the business picked up somewhat but in the end the "great expectations" were not realized. The near 3,000 in attendance at the eventful opening tapered off dramatically after the first week. The effort failed to pay and was not repeated another year. The conclusion was that proprietor Nixon had spread himself thin with his various management projects. "...Mr. Nixon has some clever ideas, but he lacks the stamina to carry them out in the same spirit in which they are conceived; he is not steady enough; he has too many irons in the fire at once, and frequently burns his fingers in the vain attempt to haul them out and work them up at one and the same time...."[155]

Hardly before the gates closed on the gardens, Nixon took Carlotta Patti under his managerial wing. The third of three singing Patti daughters, she had made her debut only a year earlier. Although she exhibited a beautiful voice and exquisite style, she was confined by a physical lameness that limited her professional career. Nevertheless, Nixon leased the Academy of Music for the purpose of re-introducing her to opera-loving New Yorkers. At the same time, he took over the management of the Boston Theatre for the 1862-63 winter season, which opened in September with the Ravel Family. Then, on October 6th, Carlotta Patti began an engagement there that consisted of five Italian operas.

Also at this time, Nixon sent a company to Washington under the management of T. Allston Brown, with plans for opening on Thursday, October 16th. A semi-permanent wooden and canvas building was erected at Pennsylvania Avenue and Seventh Street, said to

---

155. City Summary, dated August 25th, New York *Clipper*, August 30, 1862, p. 158.

be the same structure used at the Cremorne Gardens, New York, "the interior being high and dry, the seats so arranged that all can get a good view of the arena." The advertisement revealed that some 500 armchairs were taken from Cremorne Gardens for use in Washington; and that a circus marquee was attached at a cost of $3,000, over which was a balcony for promenade concerts to be given every noon and evening. But a notice abruptly appeared in the papers, announcing a postponement of the opening until Saturday, October 18th. Apparently the building had not been readied for occupancy in time. "On Saturday night the new and beautiful Exhibition Temple was formally opened to the public. The rush of patrons was extensive, and, long before the time designed for the commencement of the entertainments, the auditorium was densely packed. Hundreds were compelled to undergo disappointment, the management refusing to sell more tickets than there was capacity for accommodating the purchasers...."[156]

Nixon's advertisements were generous in their use of space and vociferous in descriptive phrasing. "Look out for the striped canopy!" "Behold the mammoth bill boards!" They identified the establishment as being "Nixon's Cremorne Garden Circus, From the Cremorne Gardens, the Palace of Music, and Equestrian School, New York, with a Full Equestrian Company and the Popular Spanish Ballet Troupe." Nixon continued to intermix art and entertainment. The initial ads made a particular point in suggesting that the interior of the

---

156. Washington, D.C., *Daily National Intelligencer*, October 20, 1862, p. 1.

building was "entirely different from the objectionable tents under which the ordinary strolling showmen are forced to give their entertainments," a statement which might suggest the presence of a tented competitor within the locality. And there was.

The Gardner & Hemmings circus was already set up on the city market lot. In his reminiscences, Richard Hemmings recalled that he and his partners decided to take a show to Washington to get money ahead for the 1863 season. They had closed the summer tour, which was by no means a banner one for most shows, on September 8th at Hanover, Pennsylvania.

> "...We opened negotiations with a man by the name of Grover, who managed a theatre there. He came on to Philadelphia to talk over our proposition, and before he left we had arranged with him to bring on our show and work on percentage basis. We had great difficulty in moving our show there, either by rail or boat, as every conveyance was occupied in transporting the soldiers, ammunition and supplies; but at last we managed to get there, and opened under a 120-foot round top where the market is now located, and we did a big business...."[157]

Presumably, both parties vied for the large number of daily visitors to the city, as well as the thousands

---

157. Al Fostell, "Richard Hemmings, the Oldest Living Showman," New York *Clipper*, December 25, 1915, p. 45.

of soldiers billeted in and around there. The Nixon camp was well-fortified, featuring the exciting *danseuse*, Isabel Cubas, as well as Dr. James L. Thayer and his comic mules, the Conrad Brothers, Barney Carroll and daughter, Charles Madigan, Charles Devere, William Naylor, Thomas Armstrong, Sam Webb, Mlle. Augusta (her first appearance in America), and the little men, Colonel Small and Commodore Foote. Also Harry Whitby, the successful horse-breaker, was there with his apprentices, Willie, Johnny, and Elvira (the latter, ironically, shortly to become Mrs. Richard Hemmings).

In order to adequately compete with the Nixon troupe, Hemmings asserted, an arrangement was made with P. T. Barnum for the services of the Albino Family, General Tom Thumb and Commodore Nutt. Hemmings also claimed that in retaliation Nixon debased Barnum in his newspaper advertisements; and, hearing of this "slander," Barnum went to Washington "with fire in his eye," got hold of the best newspaper man in town, and sent him forth to do, what the *Clipper* later labeled, "the battle of the dwarfs." With the master of publicity as a foe, Hemmings suggested, Nixon's camp soon retreated to Baltimore.[158]

Further investigation tends to challenge the accuracy of such recollections. In examining the Washington, D.C., *Daily National Intelligencer* and the *Daily*

---

158. New York *Clipper*, December 25, 1915. Barnum had been represented in Washington in late February, 1862, by his "Cabinet of Living Curiosities" which were exhibited at Franklin Hall for a few days. The What Is It? and the Albino Family were featured.

*Morning Chronicle* from September 20th through December 31st, 1862, we find no reference to a Gardner & Hemmings circus. Perhaps they were too impoverished as a relatively new organization to utilize newspaper advertising. But after Nixon's initial announcement on October 15th, an opposition ad appeared the following day. It was for Barnum's Museum, Circus and Mammoth Amphitheatre at Louisiana Avenue and Tenth Street, which was exhibiting the Albino Family, Commodore Nutt, General Tom Thumb, Old Adams' California Bears, the famous grizzly Samson, and all the members of the Great American Circus, which included Richard Hemmings and Dan Gardner in the list of performers. The same day an item appeared on page one. "Barnum, of world-wide reputation, is now daily and nightly affording our citizens an opportunity of witnessing his famous museum and circus. Thousands are rushing to see the wonderful sights which he unfolds for the amusement of young and old...."[159]

Directly, in an advertisement of October 20th, Nixon, with unabashed bravado, blatantly dropped the glove for a "battle of the dwarfs."[160]

> "A WAY TO TEST RELATIVE MERITS, and add to the fund of the Soldiers' Aid Association, the undersigned seeing a card signed P. T. Barnum, manager of Barnum's Bear Show, &c., in

---

159. Washington, D.C., *Daily National Intelligencer*, October 16, 1862, p. 1.

160. *Ibid.*, October 20, 1862, p. 3.

which he states that he has THE SMALLEST DWARF IN THE WORLD, begs leave to issue the following conditions of a challenge, to wit: 1. To place Commodore NUTT and Commodore FOOTE together on a platform in some respectable building in this city, and let the public determine which is the *smaller* of the two. 2. To allow a committee chosen by Mr. Barnum and myself, and an umpire appointed by the committee, to enter into conversations with the Dwarfs on ordinary subjects—politics, geography, military matters, works of art, foreign languages, &c., and then determine the comparative mental powers of each. 3. To allow both Dwarfs to give specimens of their performances, to show the extent of their artistic acquisitions. 4. To allow the proceeds of the exhibition to go to the fund of the Soldiers' Aid Association. 5. To show the authenticated family records of both, so that their ages can be unmistakably determined. The above stipulation I have drawn from a letter previously sent by me to Mr. Barnum, but which he has not answered. Perhaps it did not reach him; so I offer the above in order that he and the public shall see them, and in the hopes that he will accept my proposition. JAMES M. NIXON, Proprietor of Cremorne Garden Circus."

It is not surprising that Barnum, in his own defense, responded with a card in the newspaper of the following day:[161]

> "The only reply Mr. Barnum thinks necessary to make to the challenge contained in this morning's paper is that he will not aid in a newspaper warfare for the purpose of giving notoriety to an itinerant adventurer, whose only features are the "armed chairs" and a party of bogus *figurantes*, palmed upon the public as "Spanish," but whose faces have never been outside of the United States, not withstanding their pompous foreign announcement. With regard to the proposed donation to the Soldiers' Aid Association, Mr. Barnum has already paid thousands of dollars to aid the war for the Union; and he agrees that the services of Commodore Nutt, General Tom Thumb, or any other attraction which he has control of, are at the FREE disposal of the Soldiers' Aid Association whenever they hold a fair or exhibition where they may be of use to them. And Mr. B. will also present one thousand dollars to this Association whenever the showman alluded to will give five hundred dollars, after having paid up his unfortunate employés. The ladies and gentlemen who daily and nightly throng Mr. Barnum's establishment declare that never within their memory has been seen any

---
161. *Ibid.*, October 21, 1862, p. 3.

'man in miniature' worthy of being named or thought of, or who will in the slightest degree compare with these symmetrical, intelligent, and talented little gentlemen, Commodore Nutt and General Tom Thumb; and, furthermore, that they never before witnessed in any one establishment such a vast and amusing concentration of talent and novelty as are to be seen at Barnum's Museum, Circus and Menagerie. With this reply to the notoriety seeking sojourner, it is respectfully recommended that the gentleman move along to some locality where his genius will be better appreciated."

Alongside the Barnum oddities, the circus company was made up of notable artists. In addition to Hemmings and the Gardners, advertisements included the noted equestrienne, Madame Louise Tourniaire, Edwin Derious, Reynolds, Kincade, Hill, Whittaker, and a group designated the Ravel family. The Ravel family, well, maybe. Or is this another Barnum humbug?

It is unclear just who the Ravels were, for on October 25th a suggestive item appeared in the *Intelligencer*: "The wonderful Gabriel Ravel Troupe, admitted by all to be the only original Ravel organization in America, close their brilliant engagement tonight in Baltimore, and open at Ford's Theatre (Tenth Street) in this city, on Monday evening next." On the same day a card appeared as well:

"MR. EDITOR: The authorized assumption of the Ravel Family title for the purpose of dignifying in the popular esteem entertainments intrinsically mean and worthless is, unfortunately, of too frequent occurrence to challenge, ordinarily, [by] a protest from myself or any other member of the Ravel family; the more especially as that we felt certain the popular intelligence would readily penetrate the character of the fraud and appreciate its object. Heretofore these unworthy attempts to usurp the artistic reputation it is the good fortune of my brothers and myself to have acquired at the hands of the American people have been confined to vulgar and obscure bands of itinerant performers; but it is with some surprise and no inconsiderable indignation I have noted the unwarrantable deception attempted to be practiced upon the citizens of Washington by attaching the title of the Ravel family to certain performances now being given in that city under the direction of Mr. P. T. Barnum. I am unwilling to believe that a gentleman so familiar as Mr. Barnum undoubtedly is with the proprieties of the artistic world, and with the principles of fair dealing, could countenance so gross a fraud; and [I] should confidently claim from him, personally, the correction of this imposture, if but that justice both to the community and to the management of Ford's

Theatre, Washington, with whom I am about to commence a brief engagement, demand. I should thus publicly declare that the adoption of the title, or of any professional distinction of the Ravel family, is a usurpation, wholly without color or warrant. I am myself, it seems scarcely necessary for me to add, the only member of the original Ravel family now in America, my brothers Antoine, François, and Jerome being at present in France, and the legitimate representative, therefore, in this country of their professional reputation and artistic dignity. GABRIEL RAVEL, Baltimore, Oct. 24, 1862."

A reply from Barnum was quite unnecessary, for on the same page a display ad announced the last two days of the so-called Barnum's Museum, Circus and Menagerie. Following the performance on October 28th, the Nixon adversaries, Thumb, Nutt & Co., would leave the field, and Gardner & Hemmings remove to Philadelphia, where on November 24th they would open in a building on the south side of Market Street above Twelfth, formerly known as National Hall. And Nixon would have Washington to himself.

What was the upshot of this exchange of epithets between two respected impresarios? The *Clipper* suggested that the incident was an old farce, *The Pot Calling the Kettle Naughty Names*, and the cards published in the Washington papers the work of "blockheads." Yet there was suspicion that the whole thing may have been merely a publicity device making use of "the battle of the dwarfs" for, as the *Clipper* man put it, "the sake of postage stamps that look so nice and fresh in Washington." He went on to suggest that "if it is all acting, both heroes must travel with awfully muddy wheels to their war chariots."[162] But one thing is certain, Nixon was not run out of town.

Despite the disparity in admission prices between the two circuses—the Cremorne Garden Circus scaled the amphitheatre at 75¢, 50¢, and 25¢; at Barnum's Museum, Circus and Menagerie it was 25¢ to all— Nixon's advertising out-lavished and his circus outstayed the Barnum party by well over a month. From all appearances, Nixon was the victor here.

Unrivaled, the Nixon Cremorne Garden Circus seemingly prospered. Eaton Stone, the celebrated equestrian, styled the "Wizard Horseman," began an engagement on October 27th, in which he impersonated a "Comanche on the War Path." Dr. James L. Thayer was still on hand with his black-and-white mules, as were the original company of circus performers and, for a short time longer, the enchanting Isabel Cubas.

On the 31st of October came the announcement that the Washington Theatre, corner of Eleventh and O Streets, would re-open under the auspices of James M. Nixon. With Barnum and his associates gone, things must have been getting dull for the proprietor of perpetual motion. In announcing the theatre operation, he promised the citizens of Washington the "choicest

---

162. New York *Clipper*, November 8, 1862, p.239.

dramatic works," "artists of the highest celebrity," and an unequaled combination company. The season was to be inaugurated with three great stars, the "first and foremost" being La Senorita Isabel Cubas. And indeed Nixon's Washington Theatre opened on Wednesday, November 5th, with a strong dramatic company featuring F. S. Chanfrau. On the 10th Cubas re-appeared in the grand military drama, *The French Spy*, and Miss Fannie Brown was introduced in *Pocahontas; or, Ye Gentle Savage*, with A. H. Davenport as Capt. John Smith. Then, some three weeks later, on November 27th, Cubas took her farewell benefit, which included a repeat representation of *The French Spy*, in which she enacted three principal characters, with a Greek dance and a broad sword combat thrown in. With the departure of Cubas, Nixon's interest in the Washington Theatre seems to have departed as well, for on December 10th the newspapers announced a grand reopening of the place under the management of G. and F. Maeder. So ended another Nixon enterprise.

Back at the circus, things went on uninterrupted. William Conrad, the Teutonic clown, took a benefit on November 8th. On the 11th, *The Field of the Cloth of Gold* was unveiled, a piece that Nixon had previously staged at Franconi's Hippodrome to great success. The following night Prof. Haller, "adept in the mysterious arts of chemistry and rapid manipulations" appeared. The clown Jimmy Reynolds and equestrienne Marie Carroll were added to the program. Pony races were advertised for the 22nd, along with the Sherwood family, and with them, of course, the original "Pete Jenkins." More new faces were gradually added, among which were Luke and Charles Rivers, the clown Frank Phelps, and a cornet band. By December 1st, the ads were heralding a big double company. Then, only two days later, it was revealed that Nixon planned to establish a theatre in Alexandria where spectacles would be produced, replete with scenery, machinery, horsemanship and dramatic effects. It was noted that he was at present in the city and would personally superintend the direction of his affairs. The double company was divided and a portion moved over to Alexandria for opening on Monday, December 8th.

With Nixon's departure to Alexandria, the building was turned over to Tom King, the champion leaper. Still operating under the banner of Nixon's Cremorne Garden Circus and with all the appearance of Nixon's divided company, King opened on the 8th with Barney Carroll and daughter, the Conrad Brothers, William F. Smith, Mons. Rochelle, and others for a week's engagement. The lateness of the season seemed to present no problem. The weather remained pleasant and, we were informed, the amphitheatre was now being heated by patent furnaces, making it the most comfortable arena ever erected in the city. The Washington public exhibited sufficient interest to allow the engagement to be extended through Saturday, December 20th.

Then, on the following Monday, the troupe returned from Alexandria where, the advertisements boasted in typical Nixon style, "for a period of two weeks they appeared before 21,000 people." The double company apparently remained until Friday, the 26th, when Dr. Richard P. Jones, the affable circus writer, took a benefit. With that, the Nixon Washington adventure ended for the year.

In the spring of 1863, Nixon and Thaddeus Barton, leased the circus lot in Baltimore on Calvert Street, known as the "city spring lot," for the purpose of erecting a summer garden similar to what Nixon had done at Palace Gardens the previous year. But within short order the Baltimore city council rejected the plan, inasmuch as the lot was to be fixed up for what it was intended, a city spring.

Undaunted by this defeat, Nixon's organization returned to Washington again and opened under canvas May 26th on the lot at the corner of New York Avenue and 14th Street near Willard's Hotel. The company was billed in the local newspapers as Madame Macarte's Grand European Circus Combined with Nixon's Great Cremorne Troupe from New York, with twenty-five star performers. The roster included the Syro-Arabic Troupe of male and female gymnasts; the clowning of James Cooke, Sam Lathrop, and Jimmy Reynolds; Barney Carroll and his adopted daughter in a double riding act; Eaton Stone in his Indian personation on his "wild prairie steed"; and the incomparable Herr Cline on the tight-rope.

It was with this company that James Cooke, clown and all-around performer, made his American debut. The Dublin-born Cooke, whose real name was Patrick

Hoey, began as an actor in Mrs. Ellen Burke's traveling theatre, exhibiting chiefly at fairs. After learning acrobatics and feats of contortion on his own, he entered into circus performing. Subsequently, he turned to clowning, taking the great English jester, William F. Wallett, as his model, and for some time performed at Astley's Amphitheatre.

He had left Liverpool April 20th on the ship *Anglo-Saxon* bound for Quebec, but en route his ship was wrecked. Through good fortune he escaped "together with six shillings, a broken-bladed penknife, and a canary bird in a cage," which he had rescued from the sinking ship. After struggling to New York and presenting himself to Nixon on arrival, he was engaged and made his trans-Atlantic debut in the tented pavilion at the Washington opening.[163]

Still, it was Mme. Marie Macarte, with her beautiful stud of trained horses and Shetland ponies, who was the centerpiece of the circus program. Her impersonation act of the "Venetian Carnival" was featured at the beginning of the run. Then, on June 1st, the equestrian spectacle of *Dick Turpin, the Bold Highwayman* was introduced, including "Turpin's Ride to York" and "The Death of Black Bess," with Macarte enacting the role of Dick Turpin. On June 6th, the closing day, she took her benefit at the afternoon and evening performances. At this time, an additional novelty was announced for the afternoon free attraction, Mlle. Josephine Devinier was to make an ascent on a tight-rope, "walking across

---

163. Tom Cringle, *A Brief Memoir of Mr. James Cooke, Royal Jester and Circus Clown*, p. 15.

New York Avenue and completely over the Pavilion tent."[164]

The show moved next to Alexandria where they won the gratitude of Union soldiers tediously waiting to protect Washington.[165] Politicians, lobbyists, and state official were a part of the patronage despite the surrounding strife. The town was under martial law and, as enemy raids were a constant threat, no lights were allowed after a certain hour and the circus was required to close at 9:30. The stand lasted until early June when a falling off of business forced its closing.

After Alexandria, the company took to the road, opening at Annapolis, Maryland, June 15th. The show returned to Baltimore on 22nd for a three-day stand, followed by single days in Wilmington, Delaware, and Havre de Grace, Maryland, before jumping to Philadelphia at Broad and Locust Streets for the Fourth of July week. This was followed by a series of stands throughout Pennsylvania and New Jersey.[166] A week in Harrisburg proved particularly profitable, since the show arrived just as the contingent of soldiers stationed there received their pay. By this time Thaddeus Barton was business manager. At Allentown, July 23rd, the

---

164. Washington D.C., *Daily National Intelligencer*, June 1, 6, 1863; *Daily Morning Chronicle*, May 25, June 4, 6, 1863.

165. Here the *Clipper* included the names of Fanny Forrest and Ada Ogden to the roster.

166. Germantown, Pennsylvania, July 8th; Frankford, 9th; Haddonfield, New Jersey, 10th; Atlantic City, 11th; Camden, 13th; Burlington, 14th; Mt. Holly, 15th; Bordentown, 16th; Trenton, 17th; Freehold, 18th; Long Branch, 20th; Allentown, Pennsylvania, 23rd; Easton, 24th; Princeton, New Jersey, 25th; Elizabeth, 26th; Newark, 27th; Jersey City, 28th.

clown, Jimmy Reynolds, was married to Franke Christie, a member of the company. Along the way, rope-walker Josephine Webb was badly injured. She, quite likely, was the Josephine Devinier previously advertised on the bills. Finally, by mid-September, Madame Marie Macarte was posting an "at liberty" notice in the *Clipper*.

Nixon's next project was to erect an arena in New York City at Fourteenth Street and Irving Place, opposite the Academy of Music, which was opened on August 31, 1863, as the Alhambra, a name justified by its pseudo-Moorish design. The place consisted of a new 85- by 90-foot round top of canvas enclosed with the old sidewall that had been used for the traveling circus. The gas-lit arena contained a ring of standard size, 42 feet in diameter, with wooden curbing two-feet high and two-feet in width. The interior was divided into two parts, the pit and dress circle. Admission to the former was 25¢ and to the latter, called reserved seats, 50¢. The regular seating consisted of hard planks, similar to what was used by all traveling companies (although some circuses used a carpet covering on them). The boards, no wider than eight inches, were placed on uprights, simply laid on, being neither nailed nor tied. There was space between the ring curbing and the bleachers where camp stools were added when the regular seating was filled.[167]

We are again indebted to a *Clipper* correspondent for a description of the opening night program. The

---

167. New York *Clipper*, September 19, 1863, p. 171.

*entrée* consisted of three ladies and nine gentlemen, Louisa Wells, Jennie Sylvester (Mrs. William Aymar), Mrs. Barney Carroll, Horace Nichols, Barney Carroll, Jimmy Reynolds, Eaton Stone, and William Odell. This was followed by a double globe act by two unnamed performers. Barney Carroll then did a two-horse act, during which he carried William Odell about the ring. James Cooke, dressed in the cap-and-bells style of the old court fools, played to this act and made his debut to a New York audience. "...At times a person is disposed to like him for his wit, but then again he says something very stale and flat, and at once removes the favorable impression already made. He has fallen into the same error that Dan Rice has, that the audience are only present to hear him talk, and he keeps his tongue going incessantly.... His jokes are all old, worn out, and stale ones that have been peddled around the country for twenty years by every jester...."[168]

James Nicolo and his boy were introduced next in air and ground exercises, with the youngster receiving generous applause. Nicolo had come to America from England, bringing three boys, Thomas, George, and John Ridgeway, in 1853 and appeared with them at Franconi's Hippodrome in acts of posturing and acrobatics. After several seasons, the troupe returned home, where the boys became prominent as the Ridgeway Brothers. This year Nicolo was back with another boy, Bobby Nicolo, known as "The Flying Boy" (later combining with William Rodney and Thomas Tolliday

---

168. *Ibid.*

as the Talleen Brothers).

Charles Parker was next on the program with a contortion and chair trick act, which was accused of being dragged out to too great a length. The veteran, Eaton Stone, succeeded with a graceful turn of bareback riding. Then came the gymnast who was considered the wonder of the 19th century, Mons. Verrecke, a man who had astonished Europe with his feats upon the trapeze. At this time, he performed on a single trapeze suspended by a rope from the center pole.

> "...After being up there about ten minutes, and executing feats such as every gymnast in this country who makes any pretension to trapeze performances could perform, he pulls a snare drum up to him, which he straps over his shoulders, and then while sitting on the trapeze bar plays on the drum for several minutes. He then places the back of his head, or what is called the nape of the neck, on the bar and in that position strikes three taps on the drum, and his 'wonderful, exciting, and daring' performance is at an end...."[169]

In all fairness to the newly arrived Parisian, performing under the canvas roof of the Alhambra did not allow his regular gymnastic gear to be properly installed. As a consequence, his first appearance was a failure. Not wanting to continue under such circumstances, Verrecke cut off his engagement after only

---
169. *Ibid.*

a few performances and, in a short time, was placed under contract by manager James Lingard for the New Bowery Theatre, where three weeks later, on September 21st, he proved all he was represented to be. "... He is, in his peculiar exercise, unapproachable. He attempts feats from which the most daring, skillful, and carefully trained athletes have shrunk, feats which the public would consider simply impossible did they not behold them...."[170]

After a week at the New Bowery, Mons. Verrecke signed a one-year contract with manager Lea of Baltimore at a very liberal salary, making a first appearance for him at the Front Street Theatre on October 19th.

Following Verrecke on the Alhambra program were two unnamed importations from Europe who performed the Brothers Act, consisting of ground gymnastics, an exhibition which our reporter found very ordinary. He was enlivened, however, with the principal riding of Marie Carroll. "Her graceful bearing and pleasing presence cannot fail in adding greatly to the attraction of this establishment." The eleven Bedouin Arabs, who replaced her in the ring, executed a four-high posturing act and a series of somersaults that did not impress the *Clipper* representative, who exposed his disdain by labeling them "Hash Eaters who have just got their fill, and are laying down for a quiet snooze." The show closed with the performance of a trick pony, the prop-

---

170. *Ibid.*, November 7, 1863, p. 233.

erty of a Mr. Metcalf of the Bull's Head Hotel.[171]

On September 21st, young Nicolo made an impressive appearance in the Zampillaerostation act, astonishing even the hardened press.

> "...He is quite a youth, but in this act excels every artist that has ever yet attempted it in this country. He is without doubt the most regularly and beautifully formed as well as fully developed young gymnast we ever saw stripped. He performs his act with the greatest precision and coolness, and, in this act, takes the rank of first and foremost. In fact, he is about the only real artist Nixon offers to his patrons...."[172]

Throughout the stand at the Alhambra, Nixon continued to augment his regular equestrian company with visiting stars. Still, the editor of the *Clipper* found little reason for rejoicing. Indeed, he labeled the performances inferior, particularly exemplified by a young lady, Sophie Sagrino, billed as the most "daring and fearless rider in the world." She made a debut that was anything but memorable on September 14th and elicited a disdainful observation from the *Clipper*, "It seemed just as difficult for her to keep her balance on the pad of a horse as it is for a good rider to fall off."

November and cold weather arrived, hand in hand. In the face of this, the flimsiness of the Alhambra

---

171. *Ibid.*, September 19, 1863, p. 171.

172. City Summary, Monday, September 29th; New York *Clipper*, October 3, 1863, p. 195.

structure made it necessary to close up on the 2nd. In assessing this latest project, the *Clipper* man pointed out what appears to be a recurring weakness in the Nixon management style, "He opens with a great flourish of trumpets, engages a good company, promises much (performs very little of it, however), and in a week or so discharges all his best people and fills their places with inferior artists."[173]

The November dampness turned to ice for Nixon when his wife, Caroline, began suit for divorce, charging him with improper conduct in connection with an unnamed Cuban *danseuse*. The initial hearing took place November 24th before a referee appointed by the Superior Court of New York. Nixon was now faced with both an unsympathetic press and an estranged and unforgiving wife.

The next major Nixon endeavor was the opening of another place of entertainment on February 8, 1864. This permanent structure of corrugated iron was erected on the site of the Alhambra, modeled after the *Champs Élysées* in Paris. It was heated with steam and carefully designed to house winter entertainments. Described as "the new and superb equestrian temple," the place was designated the Hippotheatron. Lawrence V. Volk was the architect and W. G. Lord the contractor. The main part of the building was 110 feet in diameter and supported a dome rising to the height of seventy-five feet, topped with a cupola. The auditory was divided into orchestra, dress circle, and pit.

---

173. *Ibid.*

Orchestra seats were "armed sofas," the admission for which was 75¢; behind this was a dress circle capable of seating some 500 people, and the pit accommodating another 600. The entirety was surrounded by a hallway or promenade where standing room could be arranged. When the occasion merited it, some 2,000 spectators could be sorted and packed into place. The ring was said to be the largest ever used for indoor performances in this country, measuring forty-three feet, six inches, one-and-a-half foot larger than Astley's of London. An interesting feature was the use of two ring entrances stationed opposite each other, which allowed utility and flexibility for *battoute* leaping and the staging of spectacles.

    Nixon, at forty-four, was now at the top of his game. Odell described him as "a power and wielder of big interests." In February appreciative fellow showmen tendered him a benefit at the Bowery. But come the end of spring, Nixon suffered the loss of both Isabel Cubas and Caroline Nixon. The exciting *danseuse* and Nixon companion since her professional residence in this country passed away on Monday, June 20th. While filling an engagement at the Walnut Street Theatre, Philadelphia, she was taken ill and entered into a period of suffering from the ailment until her death. Caroline, who had been afflicted with paralysis of the side for a long time, died in obscurity a short month later, on July 20th, in Bangor, Maine.

    The seats were dusted off again and the Hippotheatron re-opened for the 1864-65 winter season on October 3rd under Nixon's proprietorship, supported by the financial backing of Richard Platt. The skilled company was comprised of François Siegrist and Marietta Zanfretta; the Sherwoods (Charles, Virginia, Ida, and Charles, Jr.); Young Nicolo, Mlle. Angelique, Miss DeVere, Miss Soyer, monkey-man Mons. William Olma (William Smith), the Talleen Brothers, William Odell, Herr Molique, and James V. Cameron (equestrian director, ringmaster and forty-horse driver). The clowns were Nat Austin and James Cooke. At this time the English clown, Edwin Croueste, first appeared, having been brought to the United States by S. B. Howes. On October 10th the great rider Eaton Stone appeared with Mons. Baptiste, the monkey-man, in *L'Homme du Bois*. James Melville and family (Samuel, Francis, and George) came on October 24th. New faces for the month of November included the performing dogs and monkeys of Henry Cooke, young Bob Stickney and his father, S. P. The great veteran equestrienne, Louise Tourniaire, was on the bill in December along with the gymnast Verrecke. A Christmas pantomime, *Harlequin Bluebeard*, was produced, with a cast that included M. Carron as Harlequin, Marietta Zanfretta as Columbine, Master Robert Stickney as the Sprite, François Siegrist as Pantaloon, and Nat Austin as Clown. The piece was replaced in February with another pantomime, *Harlequin Mother Goose*, which ran to the end of March, when the Conrad Brothers were added to the bill. The successor to the latter pantomime was *The Fairy Prince O'Donohue*, which ran until it was replaced on May 15th by *The Elixir of Life, or, the Birth of Harlequin.*

In the spring of 1865, Nixon erected a temporary building in Washington, D.C., near Sixth Street and Pennsylvania Avenue, to house arenic entertainments. The structure consisted of wooden sides and a canvas top, with a large wooden dressing area, a spacious arched entrance with a ticket office on each side, and a stage that could be inserted at short notice. The management included Nixon, William Nichols, and Richard Platt. Charley Sherwood's "Pete Jenkins" and the educated horse, General Scott, were feature attractions when the place opened on May 29th. The equestrian department was made up of the Sherwoods, William Nichols, the Delevanti Brothers, Messrs. Rivers, Henderson, Campbell, Conklin, and Smith. However, the entertainment was not strictly equestrian, since much of the program included oleo acts enhanced by a *corps de ballet.* The Ellinger & Foote Moral Exhibition—whatever that entailed—was engaged to perform in conjunction to the regular company; but the troupe remained only one week, closing on June 10th. Competition appeared in the form of Stone, Rosston & Co.'s Circus on June 8-10 at a lot on the corner of Sixth and York Avenue. After the middle of the month, business tapered off; so, closing in Washington, Nixon added John Foster, George Batcheller, and Frank Carpenter and the circus moved as far south as Raleigh, Goldsboro, and New Bern, North Carolina, the general area where Nixon had taken his railroad circus in 1860. At the latter place, coin was plentiful in the ticket wagon, the town being filled with soldiers. The show returned north at the end of July and hovered around New York City.

In the autumn, a tour was organized for visiting the principal towns of Texas by rail. The company left New York the 19th of October on the *Catherine Whiting* headed for Galveston; but after leaving port the ocean became so rough that the ship had to lay overnight at Sandy Hook. On the 23rd a heavy gale set in and the following day one of the ring horses went overboard. By nightfall all of the horses had been washed into the sea (including the performing horse, Gen. Scott, all belonging to William W. Nichols, but all ring stock was fortuitously insured). At one point, William E. Burke, the famous clown, was swept overboard only to be rescued by the *U.S.S. South Carolina.* Then, at the height of the storm, the ship's engine gave out, exposing the boat and passengers to the mercy of the tempest for a period of thirty-two hours. On October 28th the steamer went ashore five miles south of Carysfort Reef, Florida. Finally, the brig stopped at Key West for repairs, but for whatever reason may have been towed to New Orleans.[174] The circus, too badly bruised to continue to Texas, was sold or leased to Thayer & Noyes, who combined the shows into two units, incorporating the best elements of Nixon's ship-

---

174. New York *Clipper*, November 18, 1865, p. 255. The roster included Mme. Macarte, Sid Webb and wife, W. W. Nichols, the Miaco Brothers, Henry Bernard, Frank Carpenter, Frank Donaldson and son, Melville, Burt, Lyman, Devere, William Kennedy, G. Jones, Howard Duryea, agent. J. Farrell and six members were the band.

wrecked troupe. One unit, under the management of Thayer, chartered the steamboat *Ida May* and left for Shreveport on December 17th and thence to the principal towns up the Mississippi and Red Rivers. Bad fortune struck when the boat sank near the mouth of the Loggy Bayou; but somehow the circus property was recovered and returned safely to New Orleans.[175] It might be noted in passing that among the group was Charles Devere, who throughout his career received the reputation as a "Jonah," one who brought bad luck with him to the companies he joined.

\* \* \* \* \* \* \*

The year of 1866 marked the beginning of an association between James M. Nixon and Dan Castello that would continue for the next three years and carry the showmen from the East coast to the Pacific Ocean. Castello had launched his first solely owned wagon circus in 1864 when he moved into the South behind the lines of the Union army. A circus was taken out with Seth B. Howes the following year intermixing the use of the Castello title with that of Howes until the partnership was dissolved on January 6, 1866, in Memphis.[176]

---

175. New York *Clipper*, January 6, 1866, p. 311. Thayer's roster included the Stickney family, Tom King and wife, Burrows, Kelly, Campbell, Saunders, John Robinson, etc. Noyes' company consisted of Carlotta DeBerg, James Cooke, the Miaco Brothers, Jimmy Reynolds, Prof. DeLouis, etc.

176. This was confirmed by Stuart Thayer in a letter, May 19, 1996. An assertion by W. Gordon Yadon in *Banner Line*, March 15, 1968, p. 5, that Nixon was in partnership with Howes for the 1865 tour is most likely

Around this time James M. Nixon went to Little Rock, Arkansas, where all or part of Seth B. Howes' Great European Circus was stored. This was the show that had all the grand parade wagons imported by Howes in 1864. The Flatfoots (Bailey, June, Smith, and Nathans) bought part of the outfit and Nixon, Castello, and Egbert Howes put out a show under the Dan Castello name with the remainder. Castello was the manager and drawing card, Howes the treasurer, and Nixon the contracting agent. The Castello-Nixon-Howes combination opened in Memphis on January 22nd. Charles Bernard's partial routing for the season has the company in St. Louis on April 23rd, then Washington, Missouri, Jefferson City, Tipton, Sedalia, Warrensburg, Pleasant Hill and Independence, all in April. Exhibitions were given in Kansas City on May 1st and 2nd; and by the middle of August the show was in Canada.[177]

Now, Nixon, in his mid-forties, was married for the second time. The bride was Buffalo-born Emma Maddern, who was not yet twenty-years of age. We are told by T. Allston Brown that the wedding occurred somewhere in Canada. The bride's father was "a gentleman well-known in the musical profession" who had come to the United States in 1842. The new Mrs. Nixon was an actress, having made her debut at De

---

erroneous.

177. Charles Bernard, *Billboard*, September 1, 1934, p. 58. Among the troupe were Mlle. Carlotta DeBerg, Mlle. Josephine, James Cooke, Mr. and Mrs. Dan Castello, Little Dan, Charley Parker, James and Mrs. DeMott, Horace Nichols, Ferdinand Tourniaire, William Benton, Tom Shields, August Lehman, and Joe Randolph.

Bar's Theatre in St. Louis, where she had performed for three years. Later, she became known to theatre patrons in the Western cities as one of the Maddern Sisters.[178]

Castello's Great Show opened at Mobile, Alabama, March 11, 1867. It played other Alabama dates and then moved into Tennessee before proceeding north to Louisville, where it met up with the Barnum and VanAmburgh parties (owned by Hyatt Frost, Henry Barnum, James E. Kelley and O. J. Ferguson) and combined with them into one large company under the banner of Barnum, VanAmburgh & Castello's Great Show and Mammoth Moral Exhibition. This was not the whole VanAmburgh outfit, but surplus animals from it which had started from Connersville, Indiana, around April 15th. P. T. Barnum was its president; Hyatt Frost, director; Henry Barnum, manager; and Joel E. Warner, advertiser. The animal department consisted of Tippo Saib, the largest elephant in the country at this time; also, a fifteen-foot giraffe, the only one of its kind on the continent; and a double-humped Bactrian camel, royal Bengal tigers, a white Himalayan Mountain bear, silver-striped hyena, lions, leopards, wolves, sacred cattle, panthers, ibex, performing mules and monkeys, South American deer, tapir, baboons, pelicans, silver pheasants, and much more. The museum displayed some of the choicest and most popular curiosities in the Barnum collection.[179] But this seemingly formidable

---

178. T. Allston Brown, *History of the American Stage*, p. 231.

179. New York *Clipper*, June 15, 1912, p. 9.

combination was short-lived, as much of the property was withdrawn part-way into the season.

After making towns in Kentucky, followed by an incursion into Virginia, West Virginia, South Carolina, Mississippi, and back to Virginia, Castello & Co. closed in Washington, D.C., on February 22, 1868. They then settled into Frederick City, Maryland, for a respite before starting from there in the spring. In February the local *Examiner* announced that the show had arrived and "the animals, embracing a great variety, are now safely quartered at the barracks." But following the destructive fire at Barnum's Museum on March 3$^{rd}$, which incinerated all but a few of the VanAmburgh animals quartered there, the remainder of the collection was retrieved from the Castello show and returned to New York to form the nucleus of VanAmburgh's Great Golden Menagerie. On April 15$^{th}$ the *Examiner* reported that the town was lively with country people, in for a circus holiday, the show having opened their touring season on the 13$^{th}$. The street parade was judged to be a thing of beauty but "the inside performance was very poor."[180] The troupe started out under the Castello title, but by the time it arrived in Chicago for a June 15$^{th}$-20$^{th}$ stand the advertisements read "Nixon's New York Circus, Howes' United States Circus & Dan Castello's Great Show." Traveling in rented railway

---

180. Frederick (Maryland) *Examiner*, February 26; April 15, 1868, from the J. D. Draper collection. The roster included Dan Castello and Julian Kent, clowns; and the Lowande family, Brazilian equestrians, Alexander, Clorinda, Martinho, Abelardo, and Natilia; William Sparks, Herculean performer; Henry Beatty, acrobat; John Batcheller, leaper; Prof. Nash, elephant trainer; and Mr. Winners, lion tamer.

cars, the routing took them through Maryland, West Virginia, Ohio, Michigan, Illinois, Wisconsin, and as far west as Kansas. Understandably, all the dates were not made on rail. When towns were off the established lines, equipment was moved by wagons, probably commissioned from local farmers. The fall weather sent the show southward and at season's end it came to rest for the winter in New Orleans.

As early as February of 1867 the newspapers were recounting the progress of the transcontinental railroad project: "540 miles of the Union Pacific Railroad running west from Utah across the continent are now completed, the tracks being laid and trains running 10 miles of the summit of the Rocky Mountains."[181] Nixon, Castello and Howes recognized the profitability of following the steel ribbons westward and kept a watchful eye out for news of the construction as it neared completion. The new railroad was affecting a financial hustle-and-bustle in cities along the line as building and commercial expansion created jobs and prosperity. Mining towns off the rail route, where men had money in their pockets and little to spend it on, was virgin territory for traveling shows. The first circus through would reap a wild harvest. And then the moment arrived. The golden spike was driven at Promontory, Utah, on May 10, 1869. This was the signal the Castello outfit had been waiting for and, as the story has it, Nixon was on the first train out of Omaha for California. On arriving at Promontory, he

---

181. *Examiner*, December 25, 1867.

detrained and wired back for the show to come on.[182]

The stage was now set for the memorable trek to the West Coast. After opening the 1869 season in New Orleans on January 4th with essentially the same company as in 1868, and a swing through Mississippi, Alabama, and Georgia, Dan Castello's Great Show, Circus, Menagerie and Abyssinian Caravan reached Topeka for a stand on Thursday, May 13th, being the first flat car show ever to play there. The show then swiftly moved northward, arriving at Omaha for May 26th-27th, just sixteen days after the meeting of the two great railroads at Promontory Point. Wasting no time, the outfit was loaded onto an eight-car special the night of the 27th and started on the journey to Grand Island, North Platte, and finally Cheyenne, Wyoming, for May 31st-June 1st. Here the Castello troupe left the railroad for an overland trip to Denver and other Colorado locations. Along the way they encountered bad weather and muddy roads which delayed by a day the first circus company to ever play Denver. The show returned to Cheyenne on June 18th and began a trek west through Wyoming, Nevada and, at last, California, and the honor of being the first circus to play coast-to-coast.

Some have called this the high point of Nixon's career. Certainly, as co-owner and agent, his share of the accomplishment was immense. His skillful

---

182. Notes given the author by Stuart Thayer. Here Thayer states: "The story, slightly misrepresented, has been told over and over these last few years as the centennial of the trip was observed. Suffice it to say that the show had the VanAmburgh Fielding band chariot with it, from all available evidence went through Colorado, Utah and Nevada and played a month in California before being sold to Lee, High & Baker, western showmen."

hand at routing the organization is apparent. But the contributions of Nixon and Howes are obscured by the prominence of the Castello name in the show title and Castello's frequent interviews with the press in connection with the incident.

In the fall of 1870 Nixon's New York Circus was organized to commence a southern tour.[183] The South was over-crowded with circuses at this time; no less than nine shows were roaming about. Stone & Murray, and Cooper, Hemmings & Whitby, J. W. Robinson's and Stowe's were the four shows in Mississippi; both G. G. Grady and DeHaven were in Alabama; Charles Noyes' Circus and VanAmburgh's Menagerie in Tennessee; and C. T. Ames' was in the southwestern part of Georgia before he was eliminated by a bullet in Dawson, Georgia on November 2nd.

With the current war being waged on the European Continent, the demand for cotton was down, the economy sluggish, and consequently the circus business was slow. But Nixon's New York Circus had a head start on the others. Scheduled to open in Savannah, Georgia, October 3rd and 4th, the company arrived there

---

183. The company consisted of Frank J. Howes, master of the circle, and his wife Marie; the Runnells family; Sam Melville, clown; the Wambold Brothers, George and Henry, with their trained dogs; William Naylor, W. Bell, Conchita Ronzati, Minnie Wells, J. Risley, J. G. Adams, George Ward, Fred Sylvester, and the Fosters. Of the Foster family, John Foster was clown; Mrs. John, an *entrée* rider; daughter Emma, a child equestrienne; and Mamie, a tight-rope *danseuse*. Burnell Runnells and Frank Howes were in charge of the inside concert. Lafayette Nixon had the refreshment concession and the sideshow, assisted by W. McIntyre. The Albino Family and the Chinese Giant were featured. C. C. Pell was the general agent; George Stanhope, bill poster; Prof. McCann, band leader; and T. Davey, treasurer.

too late on the 3rd to give a performance but had good houses in the afternoon and evening of the following day. After making Atlanta on the 7th and 8th, the show then moved into Alabama and Mississippi until the end of November.

Head start or not, it would appear that the Nixon party was experiencing hard times. In the *Clipper* of December 3rd it was reported that the circus had collapsed and some members of the company were going up the Red River to give performances. Three issues later an item had the show exhibiting in Shreveport, on December 4th and 5th, before leaving for Texas on the 7th. Then, a letter from a Galveston, Texas, correspondent, dated January 6, 1871, revealed that "Nixon's company is here exploded, and the boys without a cent." The salaries were not paid, the circus property was attached, and Nixon was off to New Orleans. Had the "slicker" lost his gloss?

In December of 1871 Nixon resurfaced in New York City, where he opened what he called "Nixon's Amphitheatre" in a building on the east side of Broadway, opposite Waverly Place. Since its erection in 1838 the structure had undergone a variety of transfigurations and titular identities. Originally, as The Church of the Messiah, the gray stone edifice housed the pulpit for Orville Dewey, a Unitarian minister who had been keeping his hours of reverence at the Stuyvesant Institute. The Rev. Samuel Osgood became the pastor there in 1854 and the building continued in the service of the Lord until the good minister removed to Park Avenue and Thirty-fifth Street ten years later. A. T. Stewart then purchased the facility and de-sanctified it with the title of Athenaeum. There followed a rather rapid exchange of proprietorships and designations, Broadway Amphitheatre, Lucy Rushton's Theatre, New York Theatre, Worrell Sister's New York Theatre, Globe Theatre and now, for a brief period of arenic entertainment, Nixon's Amphitheatre.[184]

Nixon placed a ring upon the stage, perhaps on the very spot where Orville Dewey had held forth, and opened his small circus on December 18th. His rather distinguished company of performers included James, Frank, George, and Alex Melville; Henry Welby Cooke, George Adams, Carlotta DeBerg, Nat Austin, W. Herbert Williams, William Worrell, François Siegrist and, for her New York debut, trapezist Leona Dare. Frank Whittaker was ringmaster and Nixon returned to his former occupation of equestrian director. The arenic activity waned to a standstill by the first week in January, 1872; after which, *Cinderella* was pulled out of storage for a brief appearance.

Nixon turned to Chicago for his next venture. He leased a lot in the unburned west side of the city, on Clinton Street, between Washington and Randolph, for the construction of a pleasure dome. Work began under the supervision of Wallace Hume around the middle of April and, through the industry of the building trade, "Nixon's Parisian Hippodrome and Chicago Amphitheatre" was completed for opening Saturday,

---

184. Brown, II, p. 376-389.

May 18, 1872. The front of the edifice presented an attractive appearance with gas jets extending the entire length and an elegant arch over the entrance. A sign full across the front read NIXON'S AMPHITHEATRE! The interior was arranged with chairs in tiers from the ring to the canvas top and a commodious promenade was adorned by panels elaborately illustrated with scenes from the sports and pastimes of former years, rendered by the well-known Chicago artist R. W. Wallis. The place was lighted with gas, thoroughly ventilated, and could comfortably accommodate 2,500 people.

The industrious proprietor had grand plans for his new establishment. He envisioned the staging of equestrian, acrobatic, and gymnastic exercises, as well as elaborate productions of dramatic spectacles. The stock company was comprised of some forty performers who, the ads read, "occupied the highest niche in Hippodramatic Art and Equescurriculastiques." Oh, James! Spencer Q. Stokes was the ringmaster; Prof. Colston led the orchestra. One of the main attractions was the Yeddo Japanese Troupe. This versatile group performed feats of sword juggling, ball tossing, aerial drumming, sword ladder ascensions, and slack-wire and contortion acts.[185] George S. Cole, who was said to have a quarter interest in the firm, was treasurer,

---

185. William Worrell and James Maguire were the clowns. The Stokes sisters were there, Katie and Ella, performing their equestrienne feats; and Burnell Runnells and sons, the boys doing a double-part act; Signor Francis, the juggler; Harry and George Wambold, with trained dogs and monkeys; the Lascell Brothers on the trapeze; Charles Sherwood and son; William Naylor, Charles Seaman, and Kline & Murtz.

assisted by John Brennan; George Roscoe was the advertiser. Admission to the building was 50¢ for the parquet and dress circle, 75¢ for reserved chairs, and 25¢ for children under ten.

Nixon's promotional style remained true. For those fearful of the circus atmosphere, parents were reassured that "nothing inconsistent with the most rigid morality will be permitted or tolerated in or about the building." The proprietor stressed the advantages of comfort and permanency over ordinary traveling circuses and menageries, a promotional tactic he had used against Barnum, one might recall, in the fall of 1862. The advertisements promised this hippodramatic institution would be the largest and coolest place of amusement in the city.

He was off to a good start. On June 3$^{rd}$ he added Mlle. Geraldine and Mons. Leopold, featured double trapeze artists. Their "Lulu Sensation Act" was well received, as Geraldine stood erect on a low stage and through some contrivance was hurled into the air for a distance of around 20 feet and caught by Leopold who was hanging on a trapeze bar by his feet. Also, Commodore Foote and his sister, the "Fairy Queen," with their Lilliputian ponies and miniature carriage, were new to the company at this time. Ling Look, the fire king, and brother appeared on the 10$^{th}$. Added, too, was Prof. Chapman's trained horses, and the riding goat, Sebastian.

For a premiere production, Nixon selected *Cinderella*, which opened on the 19$^{th}$ with a cast of over seventy children, all decked out in $4,000 worth of costumes. The reader will recall this piece being a favorite of our man, he having staged it on numerous occasions. The extravaganza had been scheduled to open on the pervious day but, according to an item in the Chicago *Tribune*, a postponement was due to "the great labor involved, and the excessive expenditure."[186]

The variety acts continued alongside *Cinderella*. In addition to the usual riding and leaping, Yamadiva, the man-serpent, performed his remarkable feats of contortion, and Ling Look inexplicably swallowed his swords and ate his sticks of fire to the amazement of the auditors. Leopold and Geraldine displayed a fearless athleticism in their gymnastic exercises until they closed on the 20th and moved on to Boston. Ling Look and brother Yamadiva left two days later. Their places were taken by the popular Japanese troupe who returned on the 24th.

There was competition from visiting circuses during the month of June. Forepaugh's Museum, Menagerie and Circus opened there on the 3rd to crowded houses. And L. B. Lent's New York Circus arrived on the 17th for four days with the likes of Charles Fish, John Henry Cooke, William Dutton, and Caroline Rolland. Then, quite abruptly on July 6th, Nixon's season closed with a complimentary benefit for him. With the stable cleared of equine odors and the twenty-five-by-thirty-foot portable stage replacing the circus ring, Tony Pastor's variety troupe moved in for the week of July 8th; after

---

186. Chicago *Tribune*, June 18, 1872, an item from the Chang Reynolds papers, Circus World Museum.

which, the place was presumably reconfigured when Chiarini's circus arrived on August 5th and remained through the 24th. Three days later the Yeddo Japanese Troupe returned for another run at the Chicago patrons; after which, everything went dark.

But, as we have seen, Nixon was not a man to remain idle for long. Having experienced the success of the Royal Yeddo Japanese Troupe, he placed them under contract for a year with plans of booking them into the principal cities of the country. And he was still in possession of the amphitheatre. A New York *Clipper* ad of August 17th stressed its size and advantages, an immense pavilion, situated as it was in the best location in the city, splendidly decorated, and arranged with stage and arena, seating a potential of $1,500 nightly, available from August 26th on. Then on October 12th a new and larger ad appeared, announcing the place "thoroughly renovated and re-decorated for the coming fall and winter season." The "immense pavilion" had apparently been converted into a cozy and well-arranged theatre.

A new company managed by N. D. Roberts, under the title of Roberts' Combination, open for business on September 30th. It was advertised as "Comprising More Novelties, More Talent, and More New Faces, than ever seen together in this or any other city." The program included comic vocalist William Pastor; "Chicago's Reigning Favorite," Billy Manning; banjoist E. M. Hall; the Weston Sisters, featured in song and dance; and Miss Franke Christie, "the Best Fancy Danseuse in America."[187]

The place came alive again on December 16th when Buffalo Bill Cody, Texas Jack Omohundro, Josephine Morlacchi, Ned Buntline and company premiered an artless drama, *The Scouts of the Prairie*. Their memorable appearance has been recorded by the various biographers of Cody; all of whom relate the same questionable account of how the tenancy at the Amphitheatre occurred, but none reveal its source. With these words of caution, I recount the purported incident.

Desiring to open the play in Chicago and realizing that Nixon's theatre was the only one left standing after the fire with the necessary seating capacity, Buntline entered into contractual discussions with the lessor. He promised as a main attraction the appearance of two genuine scouts and twenty Indians. Nixon had no illusions about the merits of a play written by a dime novelist and enacted by a group of rough amateurs, but anticipated Chicago audiences would pay to see live Indians, since circuses had previously used Indian troupes to good advantage. A deal was struck. Buntline was to supply the company of performers, the play, and the billboard art; Nixon was responsible for the use of the theatre and its attendants, the orchestra, and local printing. Buntline's share of the gross receipts was to be 60%. But wait! When Nixon found out that the play

---

187. Chicago *Tribune*, September 28, 1872, an item from the Chang Reynolds papers, Circus World Museum. Others on the program were Dave Wilson, John F. Oberist, John Burk, Frank Kent, and an orchestra and brass band under the direction of Frank R. Cardella.

had not been written and that there wasn't an Indian in sight, he was furious and the contract was torn up. Not to be dismissed so easily, Buntline leased the place outright for a week, paying the required $600 in cash. He then proceeded to his hotel, hired the clerks as stenographers, and produced the piece in a matter of four hours. A bona fide Italian actress was engaged to play an Indian princess and a group of "ham actors" were picked up off the streets of Chicago to be passed off as "red skins" and the play opened on schedule to a first night gross of $2,800. After a week of packed houses the troupe of pseudo performers moved on to St. Louis and future prosperity.[188]

It has been suggested that Nixon had an interest in the company and went along on the tour. Supporting evidence of this comes from a discovery by Dr. Robert D. Pepper of a deposition Nixon gave on behalf of a Mr. Speck, who was suing Ned Buntline for false arrest. In the legal paper, drawn up at Saco, Maine, March 21, 1873, Nixon states his present occupation to be the business manager of the Ned Buntline Combination Troupe, a position he had filled since the start of the company some thirteen weeks previous.[189]

Nixon's Amphitheatre opened again in mid-March with a circus, Messrs. Clapp & Co., proprietors. The firm, under the title of J. W. Wilder & Co.'s National

---

188. One source has indicated that Nixon made arrangements for a piece of the production, but I have found nothing to substantiate the claim.

189. Notes made by Robert D. Pepper while researching the dramas performed by William F. Cody. Pepper's notes on the Chicago Amphitheater have been gratefully received by the author.

Circus, took occupancy with a troupe comprised of James Robinson and Master Clarence, Frank Pastor, LeJeune Burt, Shappee & Whitney, the Leon Brothers, the LaSalle Brothers, Tom Clifford, W. Reynolds, Albert F. Aymar, Sam Graham, Mr. Nellcourt, Nellie Burt, James Cooke, and George S. Cole, treasurer.

I now stop for a moment to take stock and consider the state of things since the triumphant tour across the continent to California. Nixon's 1870 New York Circus ran aground in Texas in December of that year. His Amphitheatre in New York City, which had opened in December of 1871, lasted less than a month. And his valiant attempt at operating an amphitheatre in burned out Chicago became an off-again-on-again commodity, one which shortly faded into oblivion. He has abandoned his New York residency for Chicago, an action for which I can offer no valid explanation; for he was a dominant figure there within the 1860s entertainment scene. And now, with his removal to a fledgling metropolis, his fortunes have declined and his trail of activity has become difficult to follow.

In 1874, Nixon's friend, Dan Castello, took him on as an assistant director at P. T. Barnum's Great Roman Hippodrome. An abandoned building situated on Fourth Avenue between 26th and 27th Streets had been leased from the New York, New Haven, and Hartford Railroad company in 1873 by P. T. Barnum, W. C. Coup, Dan Castello, and S. H. Hurd. Barnum revealed in his autobiography that the place was enlarged and remodeled; creating seating accommodations for 2,800 at an expense of $60,000, but such figures vary depending upon the source. The Hippodrome opened on April 27, 1874, as a place for equestrian entertainment featuring "The Congress of Nations." P. T. Barnum was the nominal proprietor; W. C. Coup, general manager; S. H. Hurd, superintendent and treasurer; Dan Castello and James M. Nixon, "directors of amusements"; C. W. Fuller, general agent; and D. S. Thomas, press agent. The main entrance was on Madison Avenue, the gallery entrance on Fourth Avenue. As one passed through the main entrance, the whole length of the right side of the building was filled with cages. The left side was occupied as stables for the ring stock. The parquet was furnished with cane-bottom chairs; the orchestra section, extending nearly the full length of one side, with patent iron folding chairs. A gallery of plain seats was laid out at one end of the arena; the dress-circle at the other end was outfitted with benches covered with carpeting.

In the pre-opening advertising, the Hippodrome was touted as "The Event of 1874," occupying an entire block bounded by Madison and Fourth Avenues, 26th and 27th Streets, "at an expense of nearly one million dollars." There was to be "the largest collection of living wild animals in the world," along with "The Grand Congress of Nations, the most magnificent and dazzling spectacle ever witnessed in this country," including hurdle and flat races; gymnastic acts; and pony, elephant and chariot races. Admission prices were listed as orchestra, $1; balcony, 75¢; family circle, 50¢; gallery, 25¢; private boxes, holding four, $8. A "grand parade of valuable stock forwarded by Mr. Barnum from Europe" was to occur on Saturday morning, April 25th, starting at the Hippodrome and proceeding through 26th Street to Third Avenue, to the Bowery, to Canal Street, to Broadway, to 14th Street, to Fifth Avenue, to 49th Street, to Madison Avenue, and ending at 27th Street and the Hippodrome.[190]

The press was invited to a dress rehearsal prior to the opening and a large number of prominent citizens were guests of the proprietors to preview the well publicized event. The public run-through had been scheduled for Wednesday, April 22nd, but was postponed until Friday because, while Nixon was sitting in a chariot observing an earlier rehearsal, a horse smashed into it, leaving the equestrian director severely injured. But by Friday he was able to conduct his duties with an arm well bandaged and frayed nerves becalmed. However, Dan Castello was home sick with pneumonia. And P. T. Barnum would not return from Europe until the 30th.

From a New York *Times* account of the evening, we learn that the exhibition opened with a brilliant pageant entitled "The Congress of Nations," in which most of the courts of Europe and the East were represented by embassies "accurately and splendidly attired." First in the procession came England, represented by an entry of heralds followed by knights bearing the national standard. Then came the royal carriage, on which the likeness of Queen Victoria sat enthroned, surrounded by

---

190. New York *Times*, April 24, 1874, p. 7.

an escort of Life Guards, Grenadiers, Highlanders, and knights in full armor. France was next, with horsemen representing Napoleon I and his generals, accompanied by an escort of the Imperial Guard and a company of Zouaves. After this came the Cross Keys of the Holy See, borne by a standard bearer and followed by seven guards. His Holiness the Pope entered on a chariot guarded by eight members of the College of Cardinals and followed by a deputation of Bishops. The German contingent consisted of a company of Prussian soldiers, the Kaisers Wilhelm, Bismarck, and Von Moltke being on horseback and accompanied by imperial escorts. This was followed by the "Sublime Porte," with a staff mounted on Arabian steeds and "shimmering with Oriental splendor." Italy was next, represented by a troupe of sharpshooters, Il Re Galantuomo and his staff, and a company of Garibaldians. The Pasha of Egypt and the Czar of Russia followed in the procession, after which the spectators beheld the Dragon Car, on which was seated the Son of the Moon, the Sovereign of the Celestial Empire. The Stars and Stripes brought up the rear, followed by men in the garb of settlers, a body of Revolutionary militia, a company of United States Infantry, and a tribe of Indians.[191]

The spectacle was supervened by a series of races and variety performances. There was flat racing between men mounted on English thoroughbreds; racing between men standing astride two horses; Roman two-horse chariots racing; English jockey

---

191. New York *Times*, April 25, 1874, p. 7.

racing; hurdle racing and, let us not fail to mention, elephant, monkey, and ostrich racing. Along with the equestrianism, there were various specialty acts: the gymnastic feats of Millson & Lazelle and the Levanion Brothers; Mons. Joignerey juggled cannon balls and lifted two ponies some four or five inches from the ground while hanging by his feet from a trapeze; Mons. Loyal performed on the triple trapeze; and Signor Leon, dressed as an Indian, demonstrated his skill with a lasso.

Nixon, in addition to serving as equestrian director, gave the signal for starting the races, struck the warning bell for the homestretch, and decided who was the victor, a combination of judge, bailiff and jury. The *Clipper* expressed an approval with, "James M. Nixon, the veteran circus manager, discharges his arduous duties as superintendent with an easy grace and the utmost fairness."[192]

The season ended on August 1st and the company went on the road under canvas with ostensibly the same program that had been presented to New York audiences, with road prices set at $1 and 50¢. The magnitude of the event restricted the stands to only major cities. The Boston date began on August 3rd and ran for two weeks. The company then moved to Philadelphia for another two weeks beginning August 25th. Previously, the proprietors had encountered difficulty in finding a location there, an offer for the Athletic Baseball Grounds being rejected; but, finally,

---

192. New York *Clipper*, June 6, 1874, p. 78.

they set down on a lot at the junction of Broad, Norris, and Diamond Streets. The public response was so great there that the stay was extended an additional week, closing September 11th. Baltimore was next with a September 14th opening; then a week in Allegheny City, Pennsylvania, beginning September 29th; and, finally, Cincinnati from October 13th through the 24th before the outfit was shipped back to New York City.

During the company's departure the Hippodrome building was altered for winter performances. A new roof of iron and glass replaced the canvas one and hot air furnaces were installed. The interior was redecorated, new matting laid on the concrete flooring, the railing around the interior arena was lowered, and rows of gas lights added. In the auditorium, the cane-seated chairs and private boxes on the Madison Avenue end were removed and replaced with benches, making the seating space at either end of the building available for the 50¢ admissions. Iron folding chairs, upholstered in red enameled cloth were placed on the 26th Street side, which, along with the seats on the opposite side, were scaled at $1.

The Hippodrome re-opened on November 2nd, the program commencing as before with "The Congress of Nations." That completed, Satsuma and Little All Right demonstrated feats of balancing. A flat race with five ladies followed. In turn, a small carriage drawn by ponies and driven by and carrying a pack of monkeys then coursed the arena. There was a two-horse chariot race between Miss Salisbury and Mattie Lewis. An

English stag hunt was represented by a number of ladies and gentlemen clad in hunting attire and mounted on spirited animals and headed by a pack of English hounds with their keeper. They paraded around the outer arena before entering the inner area for "the meet," which was interrupted when a stag bounded in and was at once pursued at top speed by the hounds and hunters several times around the hippodrome track. Following this spectacle, six youthful riders contested in a pony race; English and American jockeys vied for supremacy on thoroughbreds; as did Messrs. Stevens, North and Hogle in a Roman standing race upon two horses. Mlle. Victoria walked the high-wire with feet encased in baskets; then, removing them, crossed and re-crossed at a rapid gait; and closed by riding across on a velocipede.

Scenes of prairie life were portrayed by Signor Leon's troupe of Indian and Mexican riders. Indians, with their squaws, after returning from a hunt, were seen erecting their wigwams and preparing camp in the inner enclosure. While at the same time, in the outer track, there was a portrayal of natives capturing a white prisoner with a lasso and tying him to the back of a swift running horse and sending him off to meet his Maker. There was a foot race of runners wearing snow shoes, followed by an Indian hurdle race. There was a chase of a chieftain's daughter by a number of suitors, the first to lay hold of her being promised her hand in marriage. Miss Maud Oswald impersonated the Indian maiden and Signor Leon was her captor.

The sequence was terminated by the appearance of a group of Mexican riders who entered into a mock battle with the Indians and eventually chased them from the arena.

The Indians disposed of, the equestrianism continued. There was a race by monkeys mounted on ponies, a race with elephants, a race with camels; and Miss Grady and Mons. Arnaud raced with Roman chariots driven with four horses abreast. The racing over, the program concluded with a representation of "At Donnybrook Fair."

A new spectacle, "The Fete at Pekin," was introduced November 23rd, replacing "The Congress of Nations" portion of the program. With the interior profusely decorated with numerous and colorful flags, the grand procession included the appearance of a Chinese Emperor, seated in a palanquin borne by a number of Mandarins and followed by a cavalry of Tartars; and ladies of the Emperor's court also borne on litters. There were lantern and fan bearers, servants beating gongs, a winged dragon guarded by citizen soldiery and Mandarins bearing spears. After circling the track, the Emperor and his court took seats upon a platform, while the cavalry and foot soldiers performed a number of evolutions; followed by a Chinese ballet under the direction of Prof. George W. Smith, with the dancers led by Carrie Seymour and Mattie Lewis. Next, the Jackley Family of acrobats performed on a series of raised platforms placed at equal distances about the interior. The Kenebel Brothers cavorted as Chinese clowns. Satsuma and Little All Right performed feats of equilibrium, followed by Yamadiva, the contortionist. The spectacle concluded with Ling Look and his fire-eating act while mounted on the top of a car drawn by a number of horses. As the procession came to an end, a display of fireworks erupted from the car, leaving Ling Look standing amid the inferno.[193] The rest of the program remained relatively unchanged. As an incentive to draw the youngsters, a 25¢ admission for children under ten years of age was offered on and after November 30th, with feeding of the menagerie animals following on the close of each matinee.

The pantomime of *Bluebeard* was announced for the Christmas season beginning December 23rd. For the production a large excavation was made in the center of the arena and covered with a platform which contain a series of traps. A subterranean passage connected this with the dressing rooms on the Fourth Avenue side of the building. By the use of machinery below, Bluebeard's castle and other scenic devices were made to rise and sink as occasion required. A large, movable platform, made in sections, was used for the ballet dancing. And paraphernalia for the various pantomime tricks were stationed along the sides of the arena and rapidly placed into position by a corps of workmen.[194]

The extravagant pantomime included the portrayal of a Moorish village with a Turkish ballet in progress, a grand procession featuring the Great Pashaw,

---

193. New York *Clipper*, December 5, 1874, p. 286.

194. New York *Clipper*, January 2, 1875, p. 318.

Bluebeard mounted upon an elephant, etc. Bluebeard's castle arose from the ground in full view of the spectators, followed by a grand ballet. There appeared a chamber, within which were exhibited the headless wives of Bluebeard; there was the arrival of Selim and his friends to rescue Fatima and Irene; there was the usual transformation of Bluebeard into Clown, Selim into Harlequine, etc.[195] All the ingredients of a traditional Christmas pantomime.

The management made a number of adjustments following the holidays. Admission prices were reduced to 30¢ for the family circle, 50¢ for orchestra chairs, $1 for reserved seats opposite the grand stand, and half price for children in each section. This change increased the low-priced attendance but slowed the purchase of the more expensive seats. *Bluebeard* and "The Fete at Pekin" were withdrawn and the ballet corps dispensed with after January 2nd. Only the various races, the Indian life on the prairie, and the "View of Donnybrook Fair" remained. Beginning with January 14th, trotting races for a purse were introduced, which tended to revive attendance somewhat. By the beginning of February a tournament scene was added, consisting of armored knights, representing various states of the Union, with the victor crowned by a lady symbolizing the Queen of Beauty.

On February 15th a final novelty was presented, called "Salesday at Tattersall, or, Scenes Among the English Turfmen." The pageant reenacted a horse auction,

---

195. New York *Clipper*, December 26, 1874, p. 310.

showing how buyers were taken in by sharpers, all amid a background of street singers who warbled appropriate ballads. This scene was followed by a burlesque race between two broken-down steeds, terminating with police arresting the jockeys for cruelty to animals. The trotting matches continued until the Hippodrome closed on February 27, 1875.

Nixon took a benefit at the Hippodrome on March 22nd. Through Barnum's generosity he was given free use of the building for the occasion. "Mr. Nixon's well-known popularity and long career in the equestrian profession as performer and manager," a writer remarked, "will doubtless insure a large attendance, and enable him to put before the public a strong array of volunteer talent."[196]

The Hippodrome reopened on March 29th. The program at this time included two scenes from *Bluebeard*—a guard procession and a march by a group of ladies attired in armor; there were feats of balancing by Satsuma and Little All Right; a flat race between five female riders; a carriage driven around the track by monkeys; a two-horse chariot race; a Shetland pony race; a Roman standing race by Stevens, Hogle, and North; Mme. D'Atalie's cannon-ball act; scenes of Indian life; a race between English and American jockeys; a race between monkeys on ponies; a female hurdle race; a four-horse chariot race; gymnastics by Lazelle & Millson; and the whole closing with "The Fete

---

196. New York *Clipper*, March 20, 1875, p. 406.

at Pekin."[197] For the week of April 5th "The Congress of Nations" was re-introduced, with new costumes and harnesses and with chariots re-gilded. Performances were given for only the week, after which the doors were closed for the indoor season on April 10th.

This two-week reopening of the Hippodrome was merely a means of preparing for the road, a slimming-down and streamlining of the original program to make a tour of one-night stands feasible. P. T. Barnum's Hippodrome opened under canvas in Philadelphia for a week on April 12th, which served as the springboard for a six-month odyssey throughout the middle-western states. An unexpected cascade of spring rain and snow welcomed the opening-night crowd and during the early morning hours proved too much for the main tent to withstand; it gave way and buried some twenty employees beneath its folds, none of whom were seriously injured. A group of sail-makers immediately went to work repairing the damage; and, the canvas rehabilitated, the show reopened on the 15th.[198] A week in Boston began on the 17th, which was followed by jumps that took the show into Michigan, Ohio, Illinois, Indiana, Iowa, Wisconsin, and Minnesota.[199]

197. New York *Clipper*, April 10, 1875, p. 14.

198. New York *Clipper*, April 24, 1875, p. 31.

199. The *Clipper* printed the following routing: Detroit, June 28th, 29; Toledo, Ohio, 30th; Grand Rapids, Michigan, July 5th; Kalamazoo, 6th; Fort Wayne, Indiana, 7th; Logansport, 8th; Lafayette, 9th; Danville, Illinois, 10th; Chicago, 12th, for a week; Jacksonville, 26th; Springfield, 27th; Decatur, 28th; Bloomington, 29th; Peoria, 30th; Galesburg, 31st; Quincy, August 2nd; Keokuk, Iowa, 3rd; Burlington, 4th; Ottumwa, 5th; Oskaloosa, 6th; Des Moines, 7th; Iowa City, 9th; Davenport, 10th; Rock Island, Illinois, 11th; Freeport, 12th; Dubuque, Iowa, 13th; Waterloo, 14th; Owatonna, Minnesota,

Barnum's Roman Hippodrome closed the 1875 season in Cleveland on October 7th, 8th, and 9th.

Barnum had hopes of shipping the show to South America and had advertised for a partner. None materializing, he announced plans for disposal of the property of both the Roman Hippodrome and his World's Fair. The wardrobe was sold at the Hippodrome building in New York City beginning November 16th; the rest of the equipment and stock at his quarters in Bridgeport on the 29th. The animals to be auctioned off were put on exhibition prior to that date and admission prices of 25¢ and 15¢ entitled the curious locals to browse amongst Barnum's collection of beasts.[200]

For all practical purposes our story ends here. Nixon was a private man. There is no mention of him in T. Allston Brown's 1870 biographical dictionary, *History of the American Stage*, even though Brown was an apparent friend and former employee. Brown does include both of the wives, Caroline and Emma, and the former companion, Isabel Cubas. How strange. Remember, this is a man famous for his "flaming, regardless of expense advertisements," unless, of course, Nixon requested obscurity, and in so doing

---

16th; Minneapolis, 17th; St. Paul, 18th; Red Wing, 19th; Winona, 20th; LaCrosse, Wisconsin, 21st; Madison, 23rd; Janesville, 24th; Fond du Lac, 25th; Oshkosh, 26th; Milwaukee, 27t, 28th; Rockford, Illinois, 30th; Dixon, 31st; Clinton, Iowa. September 1st; Cedar Rapids, 2nd; Marshalltown, 3rd; Boone, 5th; Omaha, Nebraska, 6th; Council Bluffs, Iowa, 7th; St. Joseph, Missouri, 8th, 9th. Richmond, Indiana, October 1st; Dayton, Ohio, 2nd; Columbus, 4th; Mt. Vernon, 5th; Akron, 6th.

200. New York *Clipper*, November 13, 1875, p. 263; November 27, 1875, p. 279.

contributed to his own journey to oblivion.

There is little left on record. We know that Nixon was in Europe in the spring of 1876.[201] After two years with the Hippodrome it could have been a vacation trip. In 1879 he was said to be running a cheap theatre in Chicago. At this time he teamed with Oliver P. Myers in attempting to establish a zoological garden there. Myers was a circus agent earlier in the decade but was at the time connected with the passenger department of the Pittsburgh and Fort Wayne Railroad in Chigaco.[202] The two set a goal of raising $100,000 at $50 a share. They made an arrangement with J. M. French to use his animals, a group of that included an elephant and four lions broken to an act by Paul Schroff, which had been leased out to various circuses over the years since French's Great Oriental Circus went off the road in 1868. After raising half of the money, they were ready to present an animal display plus a summer theatre seating 4,000 people. But the day before French was to ship the animals from his Woodward Avenue farm in Detroit the barn caught fire and destroyed the lot. With only half the projected money in the bank and no animals to display, the partners abandoned the project.[203]

We know Nixon was still in Chicago in 1882, when on June 22nd he appeared at W. C. Coup's circus during

---

201. New York *Clipper*, June 24, 1876, p. 100.

202. Myers was connected with J. E. Warner & Co., 1871; contracting agent, John Robinson's, 1873; press agent, Montgomery Queen's, 1875, general advertiser, 1876.

203. Thayer's notes.

an engagement in that city. It was for a match between Tony Denier and Frank Clynes of Chicago in a four-horse chariot race with a purse of $500. Nixon represented Denier; Arthur Cambridge, a noted temperance advocate, was Clynes' second.[204] In 1886 the name of James M. Nixon was again related to the activity of Buffalo Bill Cody. A *Clipper* item announced that the "olden-day circus manager" had gone to England to make arrangements for Cody's wild west show's first trip abroad.[205] There is no word of his activities there or how long he was away; and, sadly to say, no mention of him again until Monday, September 18, 1899, when the New York *Times* carried a small item under the heading "Old Circus Proprietor Dead." "James M. Nixon, at one time the proprietor of James M. Nixon's Circus, died on Saturday of Bright's disease at the Putnam House, Twenty-seventh Street and Fourth Avenue. Mr. Nixon was eighty-years-old. His circus performed at the old Hippodrome, on the spot where the Fifth Avenue Hotel now stands. It also performed in different parts of the country and abroad. Mr. Nixon had for fifteen years past been living at the Putnam House, and was a well-known character in that locality. He leaves two daughters."[206]

---

204. Chindahl card file, Robert L. Parkinson Library and Research Center, Circus World Museum.

205. New York *Clipper*, date unknown.

206. The daughters were most likely Adelaide and Frank.

# ABOUT THE AUTHOR

**WILLIAM L. SLOUT,** an Emeritus Professor at California State University, San Bernardino, has written or edited a score of books on theatre and circus history, many of them published by the Borgo Press imprint of Wildside Press. He lives and works in Southern California.

www.ingramcontent.com/pod-product-compliance
Lightning Source LLC
LaVergne TN
LVHW041618070426
835507LV00008B/310